Helen Pagett was called to the Bar by Inner Temple in 2008. She is a tenant at Crown Office Chambers and specialises in personal injury, disease, clinical negligence and inquests, including where there are fraud and fundamental dishonesty allegations. Her practice has rapidly progressed to dealing with complex and high-value claims. Before coming to the Bar, Helen read Natural Sciences at Durham University before being awarded a Wellcome Trust Studentship to complete an MA in History and Philosophy of Science and Medicine. She then converted to law at BPP Law School. She was appointed a Deputy District Judge in 2019 and sits on the South Eastern Circuit.

A Practical Guide to Respirable Crystalline Silica Dust Claims

A Practical Guide to Respirable Crystalline Silica Dust Claims

Helen Pagett
Barrister, Inner Temple
BSc (Hons)(Dunelm), MA (Dunelm)

Law Brief Publishing

Published 2023 by Law Brief Publishing, an imprint of Law Brief Publishing Ltd
30 The Parks
Minehead
Somerset
TA24 8BT

www.lawbriefpublishing.com

Paperback: 978-1-914608-72-8

PREFACE

In the last 75 years, disease claims have generated some of the most seminal tort cases, where the most senior courts have grappled with legal issues including breach of duty and causation. Some may believe, with the passage of extensive health and safety law, disease claims are becoming a thing of the past; however, thousands of individuals continue to be injured and killed each year in the UK by occupational diseases. Silicosis, caused by exposure to respirable crystalline silica, is one such disease.

In this book, any statutes and legislations, except as otherwise stated, are correct as of 28 February 2023. Any links to websites were last accessed on 28 February 2023 and are correct as of that date.

Helen Pagett
February 2023

CONTENTS

CHAPTER ONE

INTRODUCTION

The risks of inhaling dust have been well-known for centuries. The extreme toxicity of asbestos has meant that in recent years, most personal injury claims for dust diseases have been due to asbestos exposure; those risks also being well-known to the public. While the threat posed by exposure to respirable crystalline silica ("RCS") has also been known for centuries, awareness of the risks in affected industries (and within the public generally) remains poor. It is often considered a problem of the past; however, such a perception is inaccurate. In 2014, Stonyhurst College was successfully prosecuted by the Health and Safety Executive ("HSE") and fined £100,000, after a stonemason developed silicosis from exposure to levels of silica 80 times the Workplace Exposure Limit ("WEL"). The College failed to take any measures to monitor or reduce the exposure of stonemasons to RCS, despite the sandstone they were working on containing 70 – 90% silica[1].

Despite it being known that RCS exposure, at unacceptable levels, continues today, there has yet to be the level of litigation that may have been expected.

According to the HSE:

> *"Silica is the biggest risk to construction workers after asbestos…HSE commissioned estimates it was responsible for the death of over 500 construction workers in 2005"*[2].

---

1 Details for Case No.4346892 (hse.gov.uk)

2 Silica dust – Cancer and construction – Managing occupational health risks in construction (hse.gov.uk)

However, due to under-reporting, a lack of awareness in affected industries and the medical community, the true scale of the problems caused by RCS is unknown.

Despite litigation in the UK for exposure to RCS being limited, in the last 10 years, internationally, there have been several successful class actions, including against British mining companies. There has also been recent work (although somewhat hampered by Covid-19) by the HSE, All-Party Parliamentary Group for Respiratory Health ("APPG"), and unions (including launching silica registers), which has drawn fresh attention to the risks posed by RCS.

As a result of the ongoing problems posed by RCS, in October 2022, the HSE began targeted inspections of manufacturing businesses where it is known that silica is used[3]. The inspections include targeting foundries, stone working sites and the manufacturers of kitchen worktops (where there has been increasing use of materials that contain silica). These inspections were in conjunction with the HSE refreshing its silica guidance for specific industries, including brick and tile manufacturing[4], stonework[5] and foundries[6].

For many years there has been a prediction that with increased awareness of the risks posed by exposure to RCS, there will also be an increase in personal injury claims. Recent data supports such predictions, including from the Employers' Liability Tracing Office ("ELTO"), which, in the last few years, has seen a significant rise in claimant enquiries including the term "silicosis".

---

3 https://press.hse.gov.uk/2022/10/03/hse-guidance-refreshed-to-support-brick-tile-and-stone-manufacturing-firms-to-reduce-the-risk-of-work-place-silicosis/

4 https://www.hse.gov.uk/coshh/essentials/direct-advice/brick-tile-silica.htm

5 https://www.hse.gov.uk/coshh/essentials/direct-advice/stonemasons.htm

6 https://www.hse.gov.uk/coshh/essentials/direct-advice/foundry.htm

This book has been written as a practical guide for those involved in both prosecuting and defending claims for RCS dust exposure. It is likely to be of most assistance to practitioners developing a career in disease, but it will also be a helpful overview guide to more experienced disease practitioners new to dealing with claims involving RCS. The guide is written for claims brought in the courts of England and Wales.

The book starts by discussing RCS and the known risks of exposure. It then considers the cause of action in such claims and damages. Given the long latency period from exposure to the development of symptoms in chronic silicosis, limitation is likely to be an issue in many claims, and the relevant statute and case law are considered. The final chapters focus on procedure for both pre- and post-litigation for bringing and defending such claims, including what expert evidence may be needed.

CHAPTER TWO

WHAT IS SILICA AND RESPIRABLE CRYSTALLINE SILICA?

WHAT IS SILICA?

Silicon is one of the most important raw components of the 21st Century (the late 20th Century to the early 21st Century being termed "the Silicon Age"). Its semi-conductor abilities mean that it is extensively used in computers, mobile phones and other electronic devices. By weight, it comprises about 1/3 of the Earth's crust. Silica (or, to give it its proper chemical name, silicon dioxide (SiO_2)) is an oxide of silicon. Silica is found naturally in materials such as quartz, stone, rock and sand. Different materials contain different levels of silica, with sandstone containing around 70% and marble 5%.

Because silica is found in materials such as sandstone, shale and granite, it is a major constituent of building materials such as bricks (including fire bricks) and cement. High-purity silica is also ground down into a material called Silica Flour, an abrasive used in polishes, cleaning products, pharmaceuticals (as a filler) and cosmetics. It is also used in foundry work in the production of glass and ceramics.

WHAT IS RESPIRABLE CRYSTALLINE SILICA?

Respirable crystalline silica ("RCS") are tiny particles of silica (typically smaller than 10 ɥ in diameter). They are created when cutting, sawing, grinding, or drilling any material that contains silica. The dust created is invisibly fine and naked to the eye in normal light, but when inhaled can reach deep inside a person's lungs.

RCS is generated in a range of activities and industries. The HSE, in their guidance: G404: Health Surveillance for those exposed to Respirable Silica Dust,[7] highlighted the following sectors in the UK as exposing workers to risk:

> "These *include quarrying, slate works, foundries, potteries, stone working, construction (when cutting or breaking stone, concrete or brick), and industries using silica flour to manufacture goods*"[8].

The Health and Occupation Research Network ("THOR")[9] reported the following industries and occupations were most commonly associated with silicosis in the period 2006 – 2015:

Stonemasons and bricklayers (26% of actual reported cases)

Other construction-related occupations (25% of actual reported cases)

Mining and quarrying (20% of actual reported cases)

Foundry-related occupations (13% of actual reported cases)[10]

Since silica is a major constituent of construction materials such as bricks and concrete, workers in the construction industry are considered at particular risk of exposure in the UK. This industry directly employs 1.36

---

7 https://www.hse.gov.uk/pubns/guidance/g404.pdf

8 https://www.hse.gov.uk/pubns/guidance/g404.pdf, 1

9 THOR is a network that monitors the incidence and trends in incidents of occupational diseases and identifies at risk workforces.

10 Silicosis and coal workers' pneumoconiosis statistics in Great Britain, 2022 (hse.gov.uk), 9

million people, with another 850,000 workers classified as self-employed[11].

The APPG for Respiratory Health, in its most recent report: APPG Report: Improving Silicosis Outcomes in the UK (January 2023), estimated that 600,000 workers are exposed to silica in the UK each year[12].

WHAT ARE THE RISKS OF EXPOSURE TO RCS?

SILICOSIS[13]

The most common consequence of exposure to RCS is silicosis. Silicosis is a type of pneumoconiosis, a group of lung diseases caused by the organ's reaction to inhaled dust. As with any inhaled dust, RCS enters the lungs and becomes embedded. The immune system then attempts to attack the fibres, which leads to inflammation. This gradually leads to areas of hardening and scarred lung tissue (fibrosis). Lungs which are hardened and scarred in this way do not function properly. The first signs of silicosis tend to be coughing, shortness of breath, weakness and tiredness, which are often mistaken for other conditions.

There are three syndromes of silicosis based on clinical course and radiographic pattern. The most common is "Chronic" silicosis. This is where an individual will have been exposed to RCS over a long period (usually over a period of around 10 years) at a relatively low level of exposure. The condition usually develops slowly, and symptoms can often appear 10 – 30 years after the first exposure. This type of silicosis tends not to be fatal; however, it can make individuals vulnerable to

11 JOBS04: Self-employment jobs by industry – Office for National Statistics (ons.gov.uk)

12 APPG-Silicosis-Report-01-23.pdf (appg-respiratory.co.uk), pg 8

13 Silicosis – NHS (www.nhs.uk)

conditions including tuberculosis, COPD and lung cancer which can be. It can also lead to organ failure.

"Subacute/accelerated" silicosis results from higher exposure over a shorter period (2 – 5 years). Individuals present months to a few years after exposure. They tend to be more unwell and often suffer a significant reduction in life expectancy. Finally, "Acute" silicosis is where there is exposure to high levels of RCS in a short period. The condition is often rapidly fatal. There is no cure for silicosis, and treatment focuses on managing symptoms.

COPD[14]

Chronic obstructive pulmonary disease ("COPD") is a group of lung diseases, including emphysema and chronic bronchitis, which result from inflammation, damage and narrowing of the lungs. The main symptoms of COPD tend to be breathlessness, a persistent cough, frequent chest infections and persistent wheezing.

COPD can be caused by conditions such as smoking but also the inhalation of dust, including RCS. COPD can be life-threatening. Again, there is no cure, and treatment focuses on preventing further deterioration and managing symptoms, particularly in "flare-ups" (periods of exacerbation). Treatment can include the use of antibiotics, inhalers and the use of oxygen.

LUNG CANCER[15]

Exposure to RCS can also lead to the development of lung cancer. There are usually no signs of cancer in the early stages of the disease, but as the

14 Chronic obstructive pulmonary disease (COPD) – NHS (www.nhs.uk)

15 Lung cancer – NHS (www.nhs.uk)

cancer progresses, individuals often develop a persistent cough, coughing up blood, breathlessness, tiredness, weight loss and a pain when breathing or coughing.

Survival rates vary according to many factors, including how early the cancer is detected (which is often late given the lack of symptoms in the early part of the disease). New treatments are being regularly developed, including immunotherapy; however, survival rates remain poor, with only 10% of those diagnosed living at least 10 years after diagnosis.

CHAPTER THREE

A BRIEF HISTORY OF AWARENESS OF THE RISKS OF EXPOSURE TO RESPIRABLE CRYSTALLINE SILICA

Silicosis is not a modern disease; in 400 BC, Hippocrates, the founder of medicine, noted "breathlessness" in miners. The Industrial Revolution in the UK led to the rapid development of what are known today as "occupational" or "industrial diseases". In 1843 Dr Charles Favell wrote about the well-known phenomenon of "grinders asthma" in the metal grinders of Sheffield; this would later be determined to be silicosis. The condition was named in 1870 by the Italian Achille Visconti from the Latin word silex or flint.

By the turn of the 20th Century, there was increasing evidence that many lung diseases were occupational in origin. As a result, unions pressed for occupational diseases to be included in workers' compensation schemes. In 1906 a Departmental Committee on Compensation for Industrial Diseases was appointed by the UK Parliament to consider which diseases should be added to the Third Schedule of the Workmen's Compensation Scheme[16].

In 1915 Dr Edgar Collis, HM Medical Inspector of Factories, delivered the Milroy Lectures at the Royal College of Physicians, entitled:

---

16 The Development of Compensation for Occupational Diseases of the Lungs In Great Britain, Andrew Meiklejohn, British Journal of Industrial Medicine, 1954, 11, 198.

Industrial Pneumonoconiosis, with Special Reference to Dust-Phthisis[17], which drew attention to the role RCS played in causing silicosis.

As a result of the growing awareness of risks and campaigning by unions, in 1918, The Workmen's Compensation (Silicosis) Act 1918 was enacted in Great Britain. This Act gave the Secretary of State the power to make schemes for the payment of compensation to workers in specified industries or processes who were exposed to silica dust and suffered illness or death as a result. Over the next 20 years, various Schemes and variations were made to the Workers Compensation Act in respect of compensation for silicosis.

These Schemes were the forerunner to the National Insurance (Industrial Diseases) Act 1946, which was the forerunner to Industrial Injuries Disablement Benefit. Pneumoconiosis (including silicosis) remains a prescribed disease for the purposes of this benefit.

Unlike asbestos, specific regulations regarding RCS have not been enacted in the UK. In 1997 the International Research Agency for Cancer classified silica as a Group 1 carcinogen[18]; however, it was not until 2002 that a WEL for silica was introduced by the enactment of the Control of Substances Hazardous to Health Regulations 2002. This allowed a Maximum Exposure Limit ("MEL") for silica of 0.3 mg/m^3, expressed as an 8-hour time-weighted average ("TWA"). The Regulations provided no short-term workplace exposure limit ("STEL"). (STEL is a maximum level of exposure allowed over a period of 15 minutes).

In 2006 the WEL was reduced to a maximum MEL of 0.1 mg/m^3, expressed as an 8-hour TWA; this level remains the same to date. In the USA the level is 0.025 mg/m^3 and in Australia is 0.05 mg/m^3.

---

17 Public Health, October 1915, 11 – 20

18 APPG-Silicosis-Report-01-23.pdf (appg-respiratory.co.uk), 10

In April 2020 the APPG for Respiratory Health, in conjunction with the not-for-profit organisation B&CE, following an extensive inquiry, published the report Silica – the next asbestos?[19]. The report made various recommendations including that silicosis was included as a reportable condition under the Reporting of Injuries, Diseases and Dangerous Occurrences Regulations (2013) ("RIDDOR") for those who are still at work, and to amend the Health Protection (Notification) Regulations 2010 to make silicosis notifiable through Public Health England, thereby creating a national silicosis register. They also recommended the Government introduced new legislation to bring the control of RCS into line with asbestos and the WEL was reduced to 0.05 mg/m^3[20].

In January 2023 the APPG for Respiratory Health, after conducting further inquiries, produced a further report: Improving Silicosis Outcomes in the UK[21]. Following the first report, the APPG were contacted by several industry experts who suggested there was an incomplete consideration of the risk reduction strategies within the initial report. The recommendations in the 2nd report appear to be more watered down; for example, where initially it was recommended the WEL was reduced to 0.05 mg/m^3, the later report recommended the HSE assess and determine if data and technology allow a reduction to this level. The recommendations continued to include increasing awareness for individuals who may have been exposed. It also continued

19 https://bandce.co.uk/wp-content/uploads/2020/03/BCE-APPG-silica-next-asbestos-report.pdf

20 https://bandce.co.uk/wp-content/uploads/2020/03/BCE-APPG-silica-next-asbestos-report.pdf, 4

21 https://www.appg-respiratory.co.uk/sites/appg/files/2023-01/APPG-Silicosis-Report-01-23.pdf

to recommend silicosis was included as a notifiable disease in the Health Protection (Notification) Regulations 2010[22].

At the date of publication, there have been no changes in legislation to enact the APPG's recommendations; however, the HSE continues to promote increased awareness of the risks of RCS and provide prescriptive guidance for those in control of, and those working in, industries which use silica[23]. Detailed guidance has also been produced on health surveillance for those exposed to RCS[24] including respiratory questionnaires, lung function tests and consideration for baseline x-rays.

---

22 https://www.appg-respiratory.co.uk/sites/appg/files/2023-01/APPG-Silicosis-Report-01-23.pdf, pg 4

23 https://www.hse.gov.uk/coshh/essentials/direct-advice/silica.htm

24 https://www.hse.gov.uk/pubns/books/healthsurveillance.htm

CHAPTER FOUR

DUTY OF CARE AND STATUTORY DUTIES

INTRODUCTION

It is likely most claims for exposure to RCS will be made by former employees/workers against employers/controllers of workplaces and will be brought in negligence and/or breach of statutory duty. Where there are concerns about employment status, practitioners will need to carefully consider the cause of action brought (including pleading in the alternative where necessary).

As with any personal injury claim, brought in negligence, or for breach of statutory duty, it will be for a Claimant to prove that a duty of care was owed to them, this was breached, and this caused them to suffer injury, loss and damage and the quantification of that loss.

DUTY OF CARE – COMMON LAW

Under the common law, an employer has a duty of care to take reasonable care for an employee's safety. In Wilson and Clyde Coal Co Ltd v English [1938] AC 57 the classic explanation of the duty was given by Lord Wright:

> *"I think the whole course of authority consistently recognises a duty which rests on the employer and which is personal to the employer, to take reasonable care for the safety of his workmen, whether the employer be an individual, a firm, or a company, and whether or not the employer takes any share in the conduct of the operations. The obligation is threefold, as I have explained i.e. 'the provision of a*

> *competent staff of men, adequate material, and a proper system and effective supervision"*[25].

A later formulation of the duty (following the abolition of common employment in 1945 – a defence that employees accepted the risk of being injured by fellow employees) was provided by Swanwick, J in Stokes v Guest, Keen and Nettlefold (Bolts and Nuts) Ltd [1968] 1 WLR 1776:

> *". . .the overall test is still the conduct of the reasonable and prudent employer, taking positive thought for the safety of his workers in the light of what he knows or ought to know; where there is a recognised and general practice which has been followed for a substantial period in similar circumstances without mishap, he is entitled to follow it, unless in the light of common sense or newer knowledge it is clearly bad; but, where there is developing knowledge, he must keep reasonably abreast of it and not be too slow to apply it; and where he has in fact greater than average knowledge of the risks, he may be thereby obliged to take more than the average or standard precautions. He must weigh up the risk in terms of the likelihood of injury occurring and the potential consequences if it does; and he must balance against this the probable effectiveness of the precautions that can be taken to meet it and the expense and inconvenience they involve. If he is found to have fallen below the standard to be properly expected of a reasonable and prudent employer in these respects, he is negligent."*[26]

As in many disease cases, when considering what duty of care was owed the court will be required to consider what was the foreseeable risk of harm. Given that exposure to RCS is still allowed (although limited under COSHH and only if cannot be avoided, and with appropriate control measures) the focus will be on the known risks and the

---

[25] [1938] A.C. 57, 78

[26] [1968] 1 WLR 1776 ,1783

precautions put in place – did the employer do all that was reasonably practicable?

Reasonably practicable does not mean physically possible as per Lord Asquith in Edwards v National Coal Board [1949] 1 KB 704:

> *"'Reasonably practicable' is a narrower term than 'physically possible' ... a computation must be made by the owner in which the quantum of risk is placed on one scale and the sacrifice involved in the measures necessary for averting the risk (whether in money, time or trouble) is placed in the other, and that, if it be shown that there is a gross disproportion between them – the risk being insignificant in relation to the sacrifice – the defendants discharge the onus on them"*[27].

While the fact an employer owed a duty of care to his employee to avoid injury to his health is unlikely to be controversial more difficulties arise for self-employed workers. As the HSE has highlighted, exposure to RCS is a particular risk to those working in the construction industry – an industry with a high number of self-employed individuals.

In determining if an individual is an employee or independent contractor, reference is often made to the "control test" – very simply, the less control someone has over their work, including when and how the work is done, the more likely they are held to be an employee for personal injury claims.

EMPLOYEE OR INDEPENDENT CONTRACTOR?

In Lane v The Shire Roofing Company (Oxford) Ltd [1995] P.I.Q.R, P417 the Court of Appeal considered the issue of when an individual should be considered an employee or contractor. Henry, LJ considered the "standard authorities" on the issue, namely: Readymix Concrete (South East) Ltd. v. Minister of Pensions and National Insurance [1968]

27 [1949] 1 KB 704, 712

2 QB 497; Market Investigations Ltd v Minister of Social Security [1969] 2 QB 173; and Ferguson v Dawson [1976] 1 WLR 1213, highlighted that the overall employment background had changed from when these cases were decided. While keen to emphasise that the authorities showed that many factors were taken into account and that each case is fact-specific, certain relevant principles to the case emerge:

> *"First, the element of control will be important: who lays down what is to be done, the way in which it is to be done, the means by which it is to be done, and the time when it is done? Who provides (i.e. hires and fires) the team by which it is done, and who provides the material, plant and machinery and tools used?*
>
> *But it is recognised that the control test may not be decisive – for instance, in the case of skilled employees, with discretion to decide how their work should be done. In such cases the question is broadened to whose business was it: was the workman carrying on his own business, or was he carrying on that of his employers? The American Supreme Court, in United States of America v Silk (1946) 331 US 704, asks the question whether the men were employees "as a matter of economic reality". The answer to this question may cover much of the same ground as the control test (such as whether he provides his own equipment and hires his own helpers) but may involve looking to see where the financial risk lies, and whether and how far he has an opportunity of profiting from sound management in the performance of his task (see Market Investigations v Minister of Social Security (supra at page 185)"*[28].

Where there is likely to be dispute over the employment status of an individual it is sensible for those bringing the claims to consider (and

[28] [1995] PIQR P417, 421-422

plead) alternative causes of action (in addition to a primary allegation of employer's liability).

STATUTORY DUTIES

The Health and Safety at Work Act etc 1974 ("HSWA") is the primary legislation which covers workplace health and safety law in the UK. It led to the creation of the HSE. Various statutes and regulations were passed in the latter half of the 20th Century (largely by the Secretary of State exercising powers provided to them under HSWA), which predominantly implemented European directives.

Prior to the introduction of the Enterprise and Regulatory Reform Act 2013 ("ERA"), s 47 (2) of the HSWA provided that a breach of duty imposed by health and safety regulations, so far as it caused damages, was actionable. This provision only applied to legislation which was passed under HSWA.

From a Claimant's perspective, there were significant advantages bringing a claim for breach of statutory duty, rather than in common law negligence, as the Claimant did not usually have to prove fault. The case of Stark v Post Office [2000] I.C.R. 1013 clearly illustrates this benefit.

Mr Stark was a postman. He was given a bicycle by his employers to make his deliveries. In July 1994 whilst he was riding his bike, his front wheel locked, and he was thrown over the handlebars and suffered serious injury. The judge at first instance found the defect could not have been discovered even with a rigorous examination, and this was accepted at the Court of Appeal; however, Waller, LJ held that Regulation 6 (1) of the Provision and Use of Work Equipment 1992:

> *"impose an absolute obligation, and that accordingly since the bicycle was not in an efficient state or in efficient working order when the stirrup broke, the Post Office were in breach of their statutory duty"*[29].

Mr Stark's personal injury claim succeeded at the Court of Appeal. Following cases such as Stark there was a growing perception, particularly from Defendants, that the law had tipped too far in favour of Claimants. Consequently, ERA was introduced which has led to radical changes in employers' liability law. S 69 ERA amended s 47 (2) HSWA as follows:

> *"Breach of a duty imposed by a statutory instrument containing (whether alone or with other provision) health and safety regulations shall not be actionable except to the extent that regulations under this section so provide".*

The amendment applies to accidents/injuries that occurred after 1st October 2013. Given the long latency period of chronic silicosis (10 – 30 years from first exposure), it is likely that practitioners may find that they are dealing with RCS exposure claims that transverse both pre and post-implementation of the ERA. Given this, and the fact that statutory duties will still be relied on by Claimants as evidence of negligence, below are considered some of the statutes which may be of relevance in RCS exposure claims. The list is not exhaustive and practitioners will need to consider each case on the facts, in particular, where and when the exposure occurred. Any cited statute is correct at the time of publication, but practitioners should be aware that there may have been amendments (either in the past or future) and must check carefully the legislation at the time of the period of exposure.

29 [2000] I.C.R. 1013, 1016

GENERAL HEALTH AND SAFETY STATUTES AND REGULATIONS

THE PERSONAL PROTECTIVE EQUIPMENT AT WORK REGULATIONS 1992 ("PPE REGULATIONS")

These Regulations came into force on 1st January 1993. The Regulations require every employer to ensure suitable personal protective equipment ("PPE") is provided to employees who may be exposed to a risk to their health and safety whilst at work (after the risk has been adequately controlled by other means which are equally or more effective) (Regulation 4 (1)).

The Regulations require that PPE is suitable for the risks and risks involved (Regulation 4 (2)), including taking account of the ergonomic requirements and state of health of the person wearing it (Regulation 4 (3)(b)) and it must fit correctly (Regulation 4 (3)(d)). Employees must also be provided with appropriate information, instruction and training to enable the employee to know:

> *(a) the risk or risks which the personal protective equipment will avoid or limit;*
>
> *(b) the purpose for which and the manner in which personal protective equipment is to be used; and*
>
> *(c) any action to be taken by the employee to ensure that the personal protective equipment remains in an efficient state, in efficient working order and in good repair as required by regulation 7(1)* (Regulation (9)(1)).

In respect of exposure to RCS a likely source of litigation in respect of PPE will be the provision of masks, the adequacy of them and training provided to employees in the respect of their use of them.

WORKPLACE (HEALTH, SAFETY AND WELFARE) REGULATIONS 1992 ("WORKPLACE REGULATIONS")

These Regulations provide standards for workplaces; however, they do not apply to construction sites (Regulation 3 (1)(b)) or where the only activities taking place in a workplace are for exploration or extraction of mineral resources (Regulation 3 (1)(d)). The Regulations cover maintenance (Regulation 5), temperature (Regulation 7), lighting (Regulation 8), cleanliness (Regulation 9) and other accommodation standards.

Specifically, in respect of RCS exposure, the Regulations require at Regulation 6:

> *Ventilation:*
>
> *(1) Effective and suitable provision shall be made to ensure that every enclosed workplace is ventilated by a sufficient quantity of fresh or purified air.*
>
> *(2) Any plant used for the purpose of complying with paragraph (1) shall include an effective device to give visible or audible warning of any failure of the plant where necessary for reasons of health or safety.*

A likely area of dispute in RSC claims will be the adequacy of ventilation. It will be a matter for an occupational hygienist/engineer to opine what ventilation systems should have been used at the time and if the Defendants' actions fell below an acceptable standard.

MANAGEMENT OF HEALTH AND SAFETY AT WORK REGULATIONS 1999 ("MANAGEMENT REGULATIONS")

The Management Regulations require an employer to carry out suitable and sufficient risk assessments of the risks to the health and safety of their employees when at work (Regulation 3). The Regulations require health surveillance for risks identified by the risk (Regulation 6). They also require employees to be provided with information about the risks to their health identified by these risk assessments (Regulation 10).

Claims for exposure to RCS will need to consider if the risks of exposure were adequately assessed, if employees were informed of risk, and also the provision of health surveillance as a result.

THE CONTROL OF SUBSTANCES HAZARDOUS TO HEALTH REGULATIONS – ("COSHH REGULATIONS")

The first COSHH Regulations (the 1988 Regulations) came into force on 1 October 1989. WEL for RCS were not introduced by COSHH Regulations until 2002 (0.3 mg/m^3) and then reduced in 2006 (0.1 mg/m^3).

Although the 1988 Regulations did not mandate WEL they did prohibit silica from being used for certain activities[30]; the prohibitions included, using sand or any other substance containing free silica being used as an abrasive for blasting articles in any blasting apparatus and using silica (other than natural sand) for sprinkling the moulds of silica bricks.

COSHH Regulations impose extensive duties on an employer and those in control of workplaces. At the heart of the Regulations is the principle that exposure to hazardous substances should be avoided, but where it is not reasonably practicable to do this control measures should be put in

30 COSHH Regulations 1988, Schedule 2 – Prohibition of Certain Substances Hazardous to Health for Certain Purposes

place to limit the risks from exposure, again as far as reasonably practicable (Regulation 7).

The duties imposed include assessing the risk created by working with hazardous substances (Regulation 6), preventing or controlling exposure to a hazardous substance (Regulation 7), monitoring exposure (Regulation 10) and providing health surveillance (Regulation 11).

Where a duty is imposed by the Regulations they are in respect of both employees and:

> *"any other person, whether at work or not, who may be affected by the work carried out by the employer except that the duties of the employer—*
>
> *(a) under regulation 11 (health surveillance) shall not extend to persons who are not his employees; and*
>
> *(b) under regulations 10, 12(1) and (2) and 13 (which relate respectively to monitoring, information and training and dealing with accidents) shall not extend to persons who are not his employees, unless those persons are on the premises where the work is being carried out"* (Regulation 3).

Regulations 6 – 13 of COSHH 1988 did not apply to below-ground mines in respect of inhalable dust (Regulation 5). This position was amended by The Mines Regulations 2014.

MINING INDUSTRY

Today, silica sand extraction in the UK is almost exclusively by surface quarrying (although there is one mine in Lochaline in Scotland which is underground). Coal can contain varying amounts of silica, and as such coal miners can be exposed to RCS. Although there are no deep coal mines in the UK since 2015, given the latency period for chronic silicosis, claims may be brought by former miners.

MINES AND QUARRIES ACT 1954

Again, while nearly 70 years old, the Mines and Quarries Act 1954 remains enacted.

The Mines and Quarries Act provided a duty to provide adequate ventilation (s 55) and also dust protection (s 74). Both these sections were repealed by The Mines Regulations 2014, which came into force on 6 April 2015.

THE MINES REGULATIONS 2014

The Mines Regulation 2014 was an attempt to clarify and simplify legislation for the mining industry in one set of regulations. They came into force on 6 April 2015. The Regulations specifically provided that in respect of below-ground mines COSHH must be read as if the Executive had not approved a workplace exposure limit (s 44); however, did provide requirements, at s 45, in respect of the assessment and control of inhalable and respirable dust, which specifically included reference to RCS:

> *(1) This regulation applies below ground in coal mines.*
>
> *(2) The mine operator must carry out a suitable assessment of the risk to the health of persons at work below ground at the mine created by exposure to inhalable dust.*
>
> *(3) The mine operator must ensure that the assessment is—*
>
> > *(a) recorded; and*

(b) *reviewed and, where appropriate, revised if there is reason to suspect that there has been a material change in the matters to which it relates.*

(4) *The mine operator must ensure that the exposure to inhalable dust of persons at work below ground at the mine is either prevented or, where that is not reasonably practicable, reduced to as low a level as is reasonably practicable.*

(5) *The mine operator must have in place suitable arrangements for sampling the levels of respirable dust and respirable crystalline silica to which persons at work are exposed below ground at the mine.*

(6) *If a sample exceeds the action level for respirable dust or respirable crystalline silica, the mine operator must—*

(a) *determine the reason why the relevant action level was exceeded;*

(b) *ensure that appropriate remedial action is taken; and*

(c) *ensure that appropriate further sampling is carried out for the purpose of assessing the effectiveness of any remedial action.*

(7) *The mine operator must ensure that every person who is, or is likely to be, exposed to inhalable dust is placed under suitable health surveillance, unless the exposure is not significant.*

As a result of European Directive (EU) 2017/2398 the Mines Regulations 2014 were amended by the Carcinogens and Mutagens (Miscellaneous Amendments) Regulations 2020 to remove s 44 (the disapplication of the WEL for RCS below ground in coal mines), this came into force on 2 March 2020.

FACTORIES

THE GRINDING OF METALS (MISCELLANEOUS INDUSTRIES) REGULATIONS 1925 ("GRINDING OF METALS REGULATIONS")

Although over 100 years old, the Grinding of Metals Regulations remains enacted providing prescriptive guidance for various activities where metal is ground, including glazing and cleaning of castings. While likely to have been supplemented by later health and safety legislation, the regulations remain in enforce and practitioners dealing with Claimants whose exposure has resulted from this activity are encouraged to review this statute.

FACTORIES ACT 1961

Although nearly 70 years old, the Factories Act 1961 remains enacted and provides prescriptive obligations on Factory Owners (although workplace health and safety is now predominantly governed by HSWA and regulations made under it). In respect of RCS exposure this includes the need for adequate ventilation:

> *4 Ventilation.*
>
> *(1) Effective and suitable provision shall be made for securing and maintaining by the circulation of fresh air in each workroom the adequate ventilation of the room.*

For Claimants who were employed in factories and exposed to RCS, the adequacy of any ventilation (as well as other control measures) will likely be a key issue in determining negligence.

CONSTRUCTION SITES

CONSTRUCTION (HEALTH SAFETY AND WELFARE) REGULATIONS 1996

("CHSW REGULATIONS")[31]

The CHSW Regulations came into force on 2nd September 1996. The legislation was passed under the HSWA and therefore, pursuant to s 47 (2), breach of duties imposed by the regulations which caused injuries, were actionable. The Regulations provided various duties to ensure health and safety on construction sites. The duties were imposed not only on employers in respect of employees (Regulation 4 (1)), but also:

> *Regulation 4 – Persons upon whom duties are imposed by these Regulations*
>
> *(2) It shall be the duty of every person (other than a person having a duty under paragraph (1) or (3)) who controls the way in which any construction work is carried out by a person at work to comply with the provisions of these Regulations insofar as they relate to matters which are within his control.*

In respect of RCS exposure of particular importance were the following regulations:

> *Regulation 5 – Safe places of work:*
>
> *(2) Every place of work shall, so far as is reasonably practicable, be made and kept safe for, and without risks to health to, any person at work there.*

[31] SI 1996/1592

Regulation 23 – Fresh air

> (1) *Suitable and sufficient steps shall be taken to ensure, so far as is reasonably practicable, that every workplace or approach thereto has sufficient fresh or purified air to ensure that the place or approach is safe and without risks to health.*
>
> (2) *Any plant used for the purpose of complying with paragraph (1) shall, where necessary for reasons of health or safety, include an effective device to give visible or audible warning of any failure of the plant.*

The CHSW Regulations were revoked on 6 April 2007 when the Construction (Design and Management Regulations) 2007 came into force.

THE CONSTRUCTION (DESIGN AND MANAGEMENT REGULATIONS) 2007 ("CDM 2007")

The CDM 2007 superseded the Construction (Design and Management) Regulations 1994 (CDM Regulations 1994) and incorporated much of the CHSW Regulations (at Part 4 – Regulations 26 to 44, including in respect of safe places of work and fresh air). The CDM 2007 provided that the regulations were applicable to:

Regulation 25 – Application of Regulations 26 to 44

> (1) *Every contractor carrying out construction work shall comply with the requirements of regulations 26 to 44 insofar as they affect him or any person carrying out construction work under his control or relate to matters within his control.*
>
> (2) *Every person (other than a contractor carrying out construction work) who controls the way in which any construction work is carried out by a person at work shall comply with the*

requirements of regulations 26 to 44 insofar as they relate to matters which are within his control.

As detailed above, within the construction industry a high number of individuals are self-employed. Regulation 25 provides that the regulations not only apply to employers but any contractor or person who is carrying out construction work or has control of the way in which construction work is performed. Depending on the factual circumstances, and how work was controlled and performed, self-employed contractors could still rely on breaches of these Regulations to prove a claim for statutory breach.

The ability to bring a claim for breach of Regulations 26 to 44 CDM 2007, which resulted in personal injury, was repealed by s 69 ERA (i.e. for any injuries or accidents which occurred after 1 October 2013). CDM 2007 was repealed by The Construction (Design and Management) Regulations 2015, which came into force on 6 April 2015. Part 4 remains as CDM 2007 and is likely to be relied on by Claimants as evidence of negligence.

CONCLUSION

There have been extensive changes in employers' liability law since HSWA in 1974, with the introduction of various regulations. The law has again undergone significant changes since the enactment of s 69 ERA (which will be considered in more detail in the next chapter). Practitioners are advised when dealing with claims to carefully consider the statutory position at the time of exposure and to check that this remained the same during the entire period of employment. It is also important to consider the specific industries where exposure occurred, which may be niche and uncommon, and where there may be very specific legislation in respect of RCS exposure.

CHAPTER FIVE

BREACH OF DUTY AND STATUTORY DUTIES

INTRODUCTION

Claims for RCS exposure, like all disease claims, will usually start with an individual who believes they have been injured as a result of their employment or working conditions. This often will be after a period of ill health, an attendance at their doctor, various investigations and tests, and questions about their employment history. They will have received a diagnosis, such as chronic silicosis, and been told their work history is the likely cause. Alternatively, they may have been alerted to the possibility (by their unions or other advertisements) that their ill health (possibly previously diagnosed as a condition such as COPD) may be the result of workplace RCS exposure. Occasionally, an individual may have been informed they have suffered an injury because of RCS exposure (but are currently asymptomatic) following health surveillance by their employer. The individual will then have contacted a solicitor informing them of what they have been told and what their concerns are. The solicitor will take a view if this is a matter to pursue.

It is trite, but it is for a Claimant to prove a Defendant has breached their duty (either in common law or statutorily to the Claimant). The evidence they will need to do includes:

(a) Documentary evidence

(b) Witness evidence

(c) Expert evidence

(a) DOCUMENTARY EVIDENCE

Often the first documents obtained in a disease claim will be the Claimant's medical records. This will assist in establishing if the Claimant has been diagnosed with a disease suspected to be the result of RCS exposure. They are also likely to be key evidence in questions of the date of knowledge for the purpose of limitation (which will be considered more in Chapter 8).

Claimants may often have been employed or worked for various employers/companies and there may be many possible Defendants. For those who have always been employed, the identity of the Defendants can easily be obtained from HMRC records; however, for the self-employed more investigations may be needed, including looking through the Claimant's accounts, records and diaries to try and establish who the correct Defendants are.

Pre-action disclosure (and this again will be considered in more detail in Chapter 9) from the Defendant(s) may provide documentation which goes to breach, this may include (but not limited to):

- Health surveillance records
- Testing for dust levels
- Training records in respect of PPE
- Information about PPE enforcement

However, given the long latency period of chronic silicosis, it is not uncommon for Claimants to be bringing claims against dissolved companies where there is little or no documentary evidence, in which case the issue will need to be determined on the basis of the Claimants witness evidence and any expert evidence.

(b) WITNESS EVIDENCE

The evidence of the Claimant regarding their exposure to RCS, including their awareness of exposure and control measures (including PPE), is one of the most important pieces of evidence in any disease claim. While the passage of time means Defendant(s) often are unable to call witnesses of fact; where witnesses are located, their evidence about exposure to RCS, procedures and policies in place, will be key evidence for a Defendant if they are denying liability, particularly factual allegations.

PD 32 of the CPR at paragraphs 17 – 20 provide prescriptive requirements in respect of the content of witness statements, in particular:

> *18.1 The witness statement must, if practicable, be in the intended witness's own words and must in any event be drafted in their own language, the statement should be expressed in the first person and should also state…*
>
> *(5) the process by which it has been prepared, for example, face-to-face, over the telephone, and/or through an interpreter.*

The accuracy of witness evidence (both written and oral), in personal injury claims, has been given greater attention following the introduction of s 57 Criminal Justice and Courts Act 2015 which provides:

> *(1) This section applies where, in proceedings on a claim for damages in respect of personal injury ("the primary claim") –*
>
> > *(a) the court finds that the claimant is entitled to damages in respect of the claim, but*
> >
> > *(b) on an application by the defendant for the dismissal of the claim under this section, the court is satisfied on the balance of probabilities that the claimant has been*

fundamentally dishonest in relation to the primary claim or a related claim.

(2) *The court must dismiss the primary claim unless it is satisfied that the claimant would suffer substantial injustice if the claim were dismissed.*

(3) *The duty under subsection (2) includes the dismissal of any element of the primary claim in respect of which the claimant has not been dishonest.*

CPR 44.16 further provides that where a claim is to be found to be fundamentally dishonest then a Claimant will lose the cost protection provided under Qualified One-Way Cost Shifting ("QOCS").

Fundamental dishonesty was introduced as part of Jackson, LJ's civil litigation cost reforms as a way to ensure dishonest Claimants were unable to hide behind the protection of QOCS. While fundamental dishonesty is often considered as only being relevant in low-value whiplash claims, it has been successfully argued by Defendants in disease claims, including both in respect of allegations of negligence and as a result of exaggerated claims for damages.

It is vital that Claimants and witnesses are informed of the seriousness of not providing accurate witness evidence. It is also vital witnesses make clear when evidence is from their direct recollection or is the result of reviewing records, for example, medical records.

It is important that witness evidence contains as much information as possible about:

- Working hours (including breaks and where these were spent)
- Where, at a workplace, an individual worked (including how close they were to sources of RCS)

- Awareness of exposure

- PPE, including what information was given about using and enforcement of wearing

Particularly in cases with little documentary evidence, witness evidence will be crucial for the experts instructed to deal with liability to determine levels of exposure and compliance with common law and statutory duties.

(c) EXPERT EVIDENCE

In almost all cases involving exposure to RCS, expert evidence will be needed from an engineer/occupational hygienist on the levels of exposure and if the Defendant(s) were in breach of any duty (either at common law or statutorily) at the material time. Depending on the case's value and complexity, this instruction might be on a joint basis, or each party may get permission for their own expert.

In coming to their opinion, the experts will be guided by the relevant statutes and industry awareness at the time, the witness evidence served by the parties, documentary evidence and their experience/knowledge of similar industries/activities. Where a Defendant is still operating from the same premises, where the alleged exposure occurred, the experts may conduct site visits to come to their opinion.

Cases involving exposure to RCS, like most dust disease claims, will require the experts to consider (but not limited to) issues including:

- The levels of RCS an individual was exposed to

- The measures put in place to prevent said exposure

- The control measures put in place when exposure could not be prevented (PPE, wet cleaning or time limits)

Although experts will give their opinion on breach of duty, it is ultimately for the court to determine if a Defendant is liable to the Claimant.

CONSIDERATION OF CASES

This chapter has considered what evidence will be required to determine if there has been a breach of common law or statutory duty in respect of RCS exposure; however, parties will often wish to take a view at an early stage in order to determine if they should continue to litigate a matter or attempt to settle a claim.

The limited recent litigation, in respect of RCS dust claims, means there is limited case law for parties to consider when trying to establish if a matter proceeded to court how it would be determined.

While the decision in each case will be fact specific, from case law, statute and industry guidance some preliminary views can be drawn on certain issues. The known risks of exposure to RCS, for centuries, mean any Defendant alleging they were unaware of the risk is unlikely to get far. The question of what exposure was acceptable, pre-2002, is likely to be an area of greater dispute, which will need to be determined.

The need for PPE, in particular masks, and enforcing its use appears to have been recognised from the late 1950s in respect of RCS exposure. In 1958, Parker, LJ in Wilson v Tyneside Window Cleaning Company [1958] 2 Q.B. 110, contrasted that case (where the Claimant, a window cleaner, was unsuccessful) to cases of exposure to silica dust:

> *"It is not a case that one sometimes comes across of the danger of silicosis from particles of dust which are quite invisible and cannot be seen. I do not know, but it may well be that in such cases "reasonable care" would demand that the employer should warn and exhort the*

men constantly to wear masks. But there, as I have said, the danger is not patent"[32].

The introduction of the "Six Pack" regulations in the 1990s (which brought in various regulations in respect of health and safety), which only required proof of breach, not fault, means that Claimants exposed to RCS in the period prior to 1 October 2013 may have more success in bringing claims, than those who suffered injury after this date. Claimants whose exposure includes, or is after, 1 October 2013 will still likely rely on evidence of breach of statutory duty as evidence of negligence.

How courts should consider breach of statutory duty in respect of determining common law negligence was considered in Cockerill v CXK Limited (1) Artwise Community Partnership (2) [2018] EWHC 1155 (QB), Ms Rowena Collins Rice (Sitting as a Deputy High Court Judge):

In removing the claimant's cause of action for breach of statutory duty, the 2013 Act did not repeal the duties themselves. Those duties continue to bind employers in law. So they continue to be relevant to the question of what an employer ought reasonably to do. However by enacting s.69, Parliament evidently intended to make a perceptible change in the legal relationship between employers and employees in this respect. It removed direct actionability by claimants from the enforcement mechanisms to which employers are subject in carrying out those statutory duties. What I have referred to as this 'rebalancing' intended by s.69 was evidently directed to ensuring that any breach of those duties would be actionable by claimants if, but only if, it also amounted to a breach of a duty of care owed to a particular claimant in any given circumstances; or in other words, if the breach was itself negligent. It is no longer enough to demonstrate a breach of the regulations. Not all breaches of the statutory regime will be negligent. Before the 2013 Act, the statutory regime had produced results in which employers were fixed with legal liability for accidents

[32] [1958] 2 Q.B. 110, 126

> *even where they had taken reasonable precautions against them. Stark v. Post Office [2000] EWCA Civ 64 became a well-known example. A component in a postman's bicycle gave way even though the machine had been sensibly maintained and checked; the Post Office was held liable to the claimant even though it had not been negligent. Section 69 changed that framework, with a view to producing different results*[33].

In Kennedy (Appellant) v Cordia (Services) LLP (Respondent)(Scotland) [2016] UKSC 6 the Supreme Court Lord Reed and Lord Hodge held:

> *"The expansion of the statutory duties imposed on employers in the field of health and safety has given rise to a body of knowledge and experience in this field, which, as we explain later in this judgment, creates the context in which the court has to assess an employer's performance of its common law duty of care*[34].

It is clear from the above cases that, except in the clearest cases, where even with all reasonable efforts an accident/injury could not have been prevented, a Claimant will still be able to rely on breaches of statutory duties as evidence of a breach of the common law duty of care.

This is particularly relevant in respect of WEL limits. While s 69 ERA removed the ability to bring a claim for breach of COSHH Regulations, it is hard to envisage a situation where an employer/controller of workspace will be able to argue that exposure levels over the WEL would not be a breach of the common law duty of care owed to both employees and contractors in a workplace.

---

[33] Cockerill v CXK Limited (1) Artwise Community Partnership (2) [2018] EWHC 1155 (QB), para 18

[34] Kennedy (Appellant) v Cordia (Services) LLP (Respondent)(Scotland) [2016] UKSC 6, para 64

In 2013 the HSE produced guidance for employees: Control of exposure to silica dust – A guide for employees which states:

> *"The health risks from RCS are almost entirely preventable when exposure to dust is adequately controlled – you do not need to become ill through work activities"*[35].

Claimants who develop silicosis (or other conditions) from exposure to RCS in the last 20 years are likely to adopt a similar stance, submitting that given the WEL, extensive statutory provisions and guidance in place, this should not have occurred – it was entirely preventable. While such an argument will need to be tested in the courts, one can envisage Defendants having greater difficulties in defending claims of recent exposure.

CONTRIBUTORY NEGLIGENCE

It is fairly common in disease claims for a Defendant to allege, often in the alternative, that the Claimant was contributory negligent for his injuries. The Law Reform (Contributory Negligence) Act 1945 provides:

> *1 Apportionment of liability in case of contributory negligence.*
>
> *(1) Where any person suffers damage as the result partly of his own fault and partly of the fault of any other person or persons, a claim in respect of that damage shall not be defeated by reason of the fault of the person suffering the damage, but the damages recoverable in respect thereof shall be reduced to such extent as the court thinks just and equitable having regard to the claimant's share in the responsibility for the damage…*
>
> *(2) Where damages are recoverable by any person by virtue of the foregoing subsection subject to such reduction as is therein*

[35] https://www.hse.gov.uk/pubns/indg463.pdf, 2

> *mentioned, the court shall find and record the total damages which would have been recoverable if the claimant had not been at fault.*

Given the wording of s 1 of the Act a Claimant can not be held to be 100% contributory negligent for their injuries[36].

The courts, when considering the Claimant's share in causing his injuries in employers' liability cases have consistently placed more onerous expectations on the employer as Lord Roger of Earlsferry held in Robb v Salamis (M and I Limited) [2006] UKHL 56:

> *"It is trite that an employer "must always have in mind, not only the careful man, but also the man who is inattentive to such a degree as can normally be expected" and that the circumstances which can reasonably be expected by an employer "include a great deal more than the staid, prudent, well-regulated conduct of men diligently attentive to their work": Smith (formerly Westwood) v National Coal Board [1967] 1 WLR 871, 873, per Lord Reid and Lyon v Don Brothers, Buist & Co 1944 JC 1, 5 per Lord Justice General Normand"*[37].

In respect of RCS exposure claims allegations are likely to focus on failure to wear PPE or follow instructions in terms of how to carry out work. The success of the allegations will be fact specific to each case; however, particularly with Claimants working in the construction industry, will likely consider periods of work where it is accepted the Claimant was effectively working on their own and in control of their working conditions, and also unremunerated work either on their own homes or the homes of friends and acquaintances.

---

[36] See cases such as Pitts v Hunt [1990] EWCA Civ 17

[37] Robb v Salamis (M and I Limited) [2006] UKHL 56, para 52

CHAPTER SIX

CAUSATION

INTRODUCTION

In the majority of personal injury cases, a Claimant has to prove the Defendant's breach of duty caused them to suffer injury and loss. The classic "but for test" poses problems for Claimants in disease claims and over the last 75 years there have been several, high-profile, appeals and test cases where this issue, and how the courts should deal with these problems has been considered.

The next chapter will start by considering some of these cases and judgments, and then move on to consider the relevant principles which are likely to impact on current RCS exposure claims.

BONNINGTONS CASTINGS LTD v WARDLAW [1956] AC 613

Mr Wardlaw worked in the dressing room of the Appellants' foundry, in Leith for 8 years. While in this employment he contracted pneumoconiosis from inhaling air which contained silica. The Appellants produced steel castings. The castings were made by pouring molten metal into moulds which contained sand (which has a high silica content). The castings were then annealed – the annealed casting would have some sand adhered or burnt to it. The castings were then sent to the dressing room (where Mr Wardlaw worked) to remove irregularities and be smoothed by three different machines (grinders, grinding machines and pneumatic hammers). Each of the machines produced dust, which contained silica from the sand. The dust from the grinders could be sucked away in pipes and ducts, but during Mr Wardlaw's employment, there was no way of preventing dust from the hammers escaping into the air. It was admitted that at the time of Mr Wardlaw's employment no mask or respirator had been invented to protect from this dust. During his period of employment, Mr Wardlaw's used a pneumatic hammer, outside of work, which also produced silica dust.

The Appellants admitted for much of Mr Wardlaw's employment, they were in breach of Regulation 1 of the Grinding of Metals (Miscellaneous Industries Regulations) 1925 as the dust-extraction plant for the grinders was not kept free from obstruction and was ineffective.

Mr Wardlaw was therefore exposed to both negligent and non-negligent sources of dust containing silica. At the time there was no way of knowing the level of exposure from each source. (This would be different nowadays. An occupational hygienist/engineer would likely to be able to opine the levels of exposure).

There were 2 grounds of appeal: firstly, in respect of the statutory breach, was the burden of proof on the Defendants/Appellants to prove that the dust from the swing grinders did not cause the disease, which is how the Lord Ordinary and the First Division dealt with the case. The House of Lords disagreed with this position, as per Lord Reid:

> *"In my judgment, the employee must in all cases prove his case by the ordinary standard of proof in civil actions: he must make it appear at least that on the balance of probabilities the breach of duty caused or materially contributed to his injury"*[38].

The second ground was if the admitted breach caused Mr Wardlaw's pneumoconiosis. The Appellants argued as there was no evidence of the proportions of dust emanating from various sources the Claimant could not prove the negligent source caused injury, and in the alternative, the greater proportion of dust came from the hammers and as such more likely caused Mr Wardlaw's disease.

---

[38] [1956] AC 613, 614

The House of Lords refused the appeal on the grounds that the negligent dust materially contributed to Mr Wardlaw's pneumoconiosis, as per Lord Reid:

> *"The medical evidence was that pneumoconiosis is caused by a gradual accumulation in the lungs of minute particles of silica inhaled over a period of years. That means, I think, that the disease is caused by the whole of the noxious material inhaled and, if that material comes from two sources, it cannot be wholly attributed to material from one source or the other. I am in agreement with much of the Lord President's opinion in this case, but I cannot agree that the question is which was the most probable source of the Respondent's disease, the dust from the pneumatic hammers or the dust from the swing grinders. It appears to me that the source of his disease was the dust from both sources, and the real question is whether the dust from the swing grinders materially contributed to the disease. What is a material contribution must be a question of degree. A contribution which comes within the exception de minimis non curat lex is not material, but I think that any contribution which does not fall within that exception must be material. I do not see how there can be something too large to come within the de minimis principle but yet too small to be material"*[39].

It is often, incorrectly, thought that cases such as Bonningtons and others considered in this chapter led to the development of "material contribution"; however, material contribution has been successfully argued from the 19th Century (see cases such as Duke of Buccleuch v Cowan (1866) 5 M 214. The question of apportionment was not considered in Bonningtons and the Appellants were found 100% liable to Mr Wardlaw.

---

[39] [1956] AC 613, 614

CARTLEDGE v E JOPLING AND SONS LTD [1963[AC 758

The Applicants (the Claimants), in this case were steel dressers, sued for exposure to "noxious dust" which had led to the development of pneumoconiosis. It was admitted by the Respondents (their employers) that they were negligent prior to 1 October 1950; however, the Claimants were unable to prove breach of duty after 1 October 1950. They issued their claims on 1 October 1956.

The Claimants were unaware that by 1950 they had developed pneumoconiosis; however, their lungs had suffered substantial injury. The Respondents averred the Claimants were barred from bringing a claim as they were outside the 6 year limitation period prescribed by s 2 Limitation Act 1939[40].

The Lordships had to determine if the Claimants had suffered actionable personal injury by 1 October 1950. Lord Pearce, with whom there was unanimous agreement, held:

> *"It is for a judge or jury to decide whether a man has suffered any actionable harm in borderline cases it is a question of degree...*
>
> *It is a question of fact in each case whether a man has suffered material damage by any physical changes in his body. Evidence of those changes are not felt by him and may never be felt tells in favour of the damage coming within the principle of de minimis no curat lex. On the other hand, evidence that in unusual exertion at the onslaught of disease he may suffer from his hidden impairment tells in favour of the damage being substantial. There is no legal principle that lack of knowledge in*

S 2 Limitation Act 1939 prescribed a limitation period of 6 years in personal injury claims from when the cause of action accrued or injury occurred.

> *the plaintiff must reduce the damage to nothing or make it minimal"*[41].

The House of Lords held that even though the Claimants were unaware of the injuries, a substantial injury had occurred by 1 October 1950, and the claims were time-barred. It was clear the House of Lords were unhappy with the outcome with Lord Reid making clear he would have wished to find that a cause of action did not accrue until a Claimant had discovered the injury or it would have been possible for him to discover this injury.

Before Cartledge had reached the House of Lords (as a result of the injustice suffered by the Claimants), the Limitation Act 1963 had been introduced and allowed, for personal injury claims, limitation to run from the "date of knowledge" (unfortunately for the Claimants in Cartledge while the Act gave effect in relation to causes of action which were pending at the time of passing of the Act this did not include cases where judgment had been given and an appeal was pending[42]). Limitation will be considered in more detail in Chapter 7.

FAIRCHILD v GLENHAVEN FUNERAL SERVICES LTD [2002] UKHL 22

Fairchild was an appeal of 3 cases, involving 3 gentlemen: Mr Fairchild, Mr Fox and Mr Matthews. In all 3 cases, the men had been employed by multiple Defendants and during their periods of employment were exposed to asbestos and developed mesothelioma. Only Mr Matthews was still alive at the time of the appeal, the other 2 claims being continued by the men's spouses.

---

[41] [1963] AC 758, 779

[42] S 6 (3) Limitation Act 1963

Mesothelioma is a type of cancer which usually affects the lining of the lungs (pleural mesothelioma) but can also develop in the lining of the stomach, heart and testicles[43]. The condition is normally associated with the inhalation of asbestos fibres. The condition is normally fatal (although new treatments are being developed) within 1 – 2 years of diagnosis. It is unknown what level of asbestos fibres can be inhaled without developing mesothelioma, and once the condition is caused it is not aggravated by further exposure. Although the greater the amount of asbestos inhaled, the greater the risk of developing mesothelioma.

All 3 men's claims had failed in the Court of Appeal. It was accepted if there had been only one source of asbestos (one Defendant) the men's claims succeeded – they could satisfy the "but for test"; however, their claims had previously failed because there were multiple Defendants, but they could not prove (because it was scientifically unproveable) causation against a specific Defendant.

All 3 claims succeeded in the House of Lords which allowed a "modified approach" to causation where there was a material risk of contracting a disease in specific circumstances, namely that:

- The Claimant was negligently exposed to a noxious agent by multiple Defendants (in Fairchild it was asbestos, but would equally apply to RCS)
- Each exposure increased the risk of developing the disease
- Causes other than the tortious exposure can effectively be discounted
- Science does not enable attribution or apportionment between the Defendants

43 https://www.nhs.uk/conditions/mesothelioma/

Lord Bingham was keen to emphasise it was only when all those criteria were met a Claimant could succeed:

> *"I would in conclusion emphasise that my opinion is directed to cases in which each of the conditions specified in (1) – (6) of paragraph 2 above is satisfied and to no other case. It would be unrealistic to suppose that the principle here affirmed will not over time be the subject of incremental and analogical development. Cases seeking to develop the principle must be decided when and as they arise. For the present, I think it unwise to decide more than is necessary to resolve these three appeals which, for all the foregoing reasons, I concluded should be allowed"*[44].

Apportionment was not argued at the Appeal, but shortly was, in the matters of Holtby v Brigham and Cowan (Hull) Ltd [2000] EWCA Civ 111 and Barker v Corus (Plc) [2006] UKHL 20.

HOLTBY V BRIGHAM AND COWAN (HULL) LTD [2000] EWCA CIV 111

Mr Holtby, a marine fitter, developed asbestosis after being exposed to asbestos during the course of his working life. For approximately 12 years he was employed by the Defendants. For the remaining 27 years, he was employed by other employers, including some he spent quite long periods with (4 and 5 years).

The Defendants at first instance, successfully, argued they should only be liable to the extent that they contributed towards the disability. The Claimant appealed arguing as the Defendant's conduct materially contributed to the asbestosis he can recover all his loss from them (relying on the decision in Bonningtons).

[44] [2002] UKHL 22, para 34

The Claimant's appeal failed. The Court holding that the Claimant will succeed if he can prove the Defendant's negligent conduct materially contributed to his disability, but the Defendant would only be liable for that contribution; however, if that argument is not pleaded or argued by the Defendant the Claimant will succeed in full (as they did in Bonningtons).

BARKER v CORUS (UK) PLC [2006] UKHL PLC

The House of Lords considered 3 appeals. All the gentlemen had died of mesothelioma by the time of the Appeal and the claims were brought on behalf of their estates and for dependents. In Mr Baker's case it was agreed the Claimant had had 3 material exposures to asbestos during his working career, 2 were as a result of a breach of duty by his employers and the third it was accepted involved a failure by Mr Baker to take care for his own safety. One of the 2 employers, Graessers Ltd, was insolvent with no identifiable insurer. At first instance, and approved by the Court of Appeal, the court held Corus (UK) Plc were joint and severally liable with Graessers Ltd to Mr Baker, and as such were liable for 80% of the claim (the court awarding a discount of 20% for the contributory negligence of Mr Baker).

In the other 2 appeals there was no dispute that the exposures by employers and occupiers were negligent and fell within the exception in Fairchild. In both appeals some of the employers were insolvent and uninsured and some were not. The Court of Appeal held all the employers were joint and severally liable. The result was in the case involving the late Mr Patterson, 2 solvent companies, who accounted for 16.78% of the Deceased's exposure to asbestos were equally liable for 100% of the claim. In the case of the late Mr Murray, the 5 solvent Defendants accounted for 42.5% of the period of exposure but were liable for 100% of the claim.

The Defendants in all 3 cases appealed on the grounds they should be severally liable and as such only liable for the period of exposure which they caused.

The House of Lords allowed all 3 claims holding as per Lord Scott of Foscott:

> *"the extent of the liability of each defendant in a Fairchild type of case, where it cannot be shown which defendant's breach of duty caused the damage but where each defendant, in breach of duty, has exposed the claimant to a significant risk of the eventual damage, should be liability commensurate with the degree of risk for which that defendant was responsible. Ascertainment of the degree of risk would be an issue of fact to be determined by the trial judge. The issue would depend upon the duration of the exposure for which each negligent defendant was responsible compared with the total duration of the claimant's exposure to the injurious agent in question. It might depend also on the intensity of the exposure for which the defendant was responsible compared with the intensity of the exposure for which the defendant was not responsible. The exact type of agent might be a relevant factor in assessing the degree of risk. I have in mind that there are different types of asbestos and some might create a greater risk than others. Other factors relevant to the degree of risk might come into the picture as well. The assessment of the percentage risk for which an individual defendant was responsible, and therefore the percentage of the total damage for which that defendant could be held liable, would, as I have said, be an issue of fact to be decided on the evidence in each case"*[45]:

Following this decision, there was a significant backlash from unions and victims of asbestos exposure. This swiftly led to the introduction of the Compensation Act 2006, of which s 3 provides that a person who has negligently or in breach of statutory duty permitted a victim to be

45 [2006] UKHL PLC, paragraph 62

exposed to asbestos, and that victim develops mesothelioma, is liable in respect of the whole of the damage.

JOHNSTON v NEI INTERNATIONAL COMBUSTION LTD, ROTHWELL V CHEMICAL AND INSULATING CO LTD [2008] AC 281

The question of actionable damage was considered in Johnston, Rothwell. 10 test cases were taken to the House of Lords in what is known as the "Pleural Plaque Litigation". The various appeals were all on the question of if negligent exposure to asbestos during employment, which causes pleural plaques, is actional damage for which a Defendant will be liable. Pleural plaques cause areas of fibrous thickening of the pleural membrane, which in all but the most exceptional of cases causes no symptoms and does not increase the risk of developing other diseases. They do indicate, however, an individual has been exposed to asbestos and therefore may develop asbestos-related conditions in the future (but the presence of pleural plaques gives no indication if this will occur, or which disease may develop (if any)).

Additionally, in one appeal, involving a Mr Grieves, the court also had to consider whether the Defendant owed him a duty of care in respect of the development of anxiety as the result of developing pleural plaques, and therefore being aware he had been exposed to asbestos and therefore could develop conditions like mesothelioma in the future.

The court, in giving judgment, considered and distinguished the decision in Cartledge and decided that asymptomatic pleural plaques did not constitute an injury which gave rise to a claim for damages in tort. As per Lord Hoffman:

> *"A claim in tort based on negligence is incomplete without proof of damage. Damage in this sense is an abstract concept of being worse off, physically or economically, so that compensation is an appropriate remedy…How much worse off must one be? An action for*

compensation should not be set in motion on account of a trivial injury. De minimis non curat lex. But whether an injury is sufficiently serious to found a claim for compensation or too trivial to justify a remedy is a question of degree... [In] Cartledge v E Jopling and Sons Ltd [1963] AC 758...At a date earlier than the commencement of the limitation period their lungs had suffered damage which would have been visible on an X-ray examination, reduced their lung capacity in a way which would show itself in cases of unusual exertion, might advance without further inhalation, made them more vulnerable to tuberculosis or bronchitis and reduced their expectation of life. But in normal life the damage produced no symptoms and they were unaware of it. The House of Lords affirmed the view of the trial judge and the Court of Appeal that a cause of action had arisen[46]*".*

The difference between actionable damage (like in Cartledge) and non-actionable damage (pleural plaques) appears to be that pleural plaques were found to be neutral in terms health impacts, they would not cause symptoms, they did not increase the susceptibility to other disease and did not reduce life expectancy. This can be contrasted with the Claimants in Cartledge where the evidence was the damage suffered (even before the Claimants were aware) would have left the individuals more vulnerable to other diseases and reduced their life expectancy.

Mr Grieves appeal also failed. The House of Lords holding that it was not reasonably foreseeable that as a result of creating the risk of an asbestos-related disease an individual of reasonable fortitude will develop a psychiatric injury.

[46] [2008] AC 281, para 8

SIENKIEWICZ V GRIEF (UK) LTD [2011] UKSC 10

In Sienkiewicz the Deceased (a Mrs Costello) died from mesothelioma in 2006. Between 1966 until 1984 she worked in an office where asbestos dust was released into the factory atmosphere (it was accepted this was negligent). Like all residents in the area, she would have also been exposed to low levels of asbestos in the general atmosphere (non-negligent). The Defendant argued that the Fairchild exception did not apply in this case because this was a "single exposure" case, as the Defendant was the only known source of occupational exposure, and accordingly the appropriate causation test was the "double the risk" test. (The "double the risk" test is often cited as the threshold that a Claimant needs to get over to bring a claim for an increased risk of an indivisible disease. The "double the risk" test applies epidemiological data to determine causation, where medical science cannot do so, and where, if the statistical evidence supports that the tortfeasor doubled the risk of the victim developing the disease then it follows it is more likely than not that they caused the injury.)

The Defendants submitted that only if exposure could have been shown to double the risk could they be liable. At first instance, the judge found the occupational exposure only increased the risk of developing mesothelioma by 18% and as such the claim failed. The Court of Appeal reversed this decision finding that the proper test was if the occupational exposure had materially increased the risk of contracting the disease. The Defendant appealed.

The Supreme Court dismissed the appeal. They considered the double the risk test was unsuitable as a test for causation in mesothelioma cases. The Court was satisfied in Mrs Costello's case, that the occupational exposure materially increased the Deceased's risk of developing mesothelioma.

HENEGHAN V MANCHESTER DRY DOCKS LIMITED [2016] EWCA CIV 86

Mr Heneghan died from asbestos-related lung cancer in January 2013. He was exposed to asbestos in the period 1961 – 1974 by 10 different employers. The Claimant sued 6 of the employers. Science could still not establish which, if any, of the exposures triggered the Claimant's lung cancer; however, epidemiological and statistical evidence could establish by how much each exposure had increased the risk of contracting the disease.

As S 3 of Compensation Act 2006 only applies to Mesothelioma claims, the Defendant successfully argued, at first instance, that damages against each Defendant should be awarded in proportion to the risk they were responsible for (in line with Barker). The outcome was that the Claimant's estate and his widow only recovered 32.5% of the claim (£61,600 versus £175,000). The Claimant appealed the decision on the basis each Defendant had materially contributed to the cancer and was therefore liable for damages in full.

The Court of Appeal looked more favourably on the "double risk" test in this case, the application of which evidenced that the Deceased's risk of developing lung care had been increased by over 5 times as a result of asbestos exposure. Medical science could not however determine which of the Defendant's exposure caused the Claimant's cancer. It was also common ground that exposure attributable to any of the pursued individual Defendants could not be proved to have doubled the risk the Deceased would develop lung-cancer.

The Court of Appeal upheld the first instance decision of Jay, J ([2014] EWHC 4190 QB) who held at paragraph 63:

> *"In my judgment, it makes no sense in this sort of case to say that each Defendant's exposures materially contributed to the disease process, invoking the second limb of Lord Reid's formulation in Bonnington Castings. Adopting Lord Reid's approach in McGhee, the evidence does*

> *not establish that every asbestos fibre, or exposure, was or must have been implicated in the disease process. The aetiology of lung cancer is different from silicosis or pneumoconiosis. In those cases, which depend on the gradual accumulation of lung dust, the disease process is continuous and the concept of material contribution has an intelligible role. In lung cancer cases, there is no analogue to the gradual accumulation in the lungs of asbestos or cigarette smoke. The risk of the disease eventuating is proportionate to the quantum of exposure, but that is a statistical judgment, not an assessment which may be linked to the physical presence of deposits of dust in the lung".*

Accordingly, apportionment was required between the Defendants and damages were awarded on that basis.

WHAT PRINCIPLES CAN PRACTITIONERS DRAW FROM THESE CASES?

A practitioner, looking at the above cases, may feel somewhat overwhelmed about what principles can be drawn from them and how they apply to their specific cases of RCS exposure. The Master of Rolls, in Heneghan helpfully summarised that there are 3 ways of establishing causation:

> *"The first is by showing that but for the defendant's negligence, the claimant would not have suffered the disease. Secondly, where the disease is caused by the cumulative effect of an agency part of which is attributable to breach of duty on the part of the defendant and part of which involves no breach of duty, the defendant will be liable on the ground that his breach of duty made a "material contribution" to the disease: Bonnington Castings Ltd v Wardlaw [1956] AC 613. The disease in that case was pneumoconiosis which is a divisible disease (i.e. one whose severity increases with increased exposure to the agency). Thirdly, where causation cannot be proved in either of these ways, for example because the disease is indivisible, causation may be established*

if it is proved that the defendant materially increased the risk of the victim contracting the disease: the Fairchild exception"[47].

The first thing a practitioner needs to consider is: has actionable damage be suffered?

ACTIONABLE DAMAGE

Where a Claimant has been diagnosed with a disease such as silicosis or lung cancer there will be no issue in establishing the Claimant has suffered "actionable damage"; however,

with increased health surveillance it is possible that individuals may become aware of changes in their lungs (for example thickening), which will likely have been caused by exposure to RCS; however, the Claimant is asymptomatic. The question arises would this constitute a compensable injury? Additionally, where a Claimant's symptoms are minimal Defendants may raise "de minimis non curat lex" (the law does not take account of trifling matters).

As per Lord Pearce in Cartledge the question of actionable harm is one of fact. Where a Claimant can prove even where they are asymptomatic, an injury, will cause an increased risk of other diseases, or reduced life expectancy, they are likely to be successful in proving they have suffered actionable damage.

Where a practitioner has concerns on this issue it will be important to obtain expert medical evidence if an injury will deteriorate in future, if it will increase the risk of certain diseases and reduce life expectancy.

[47] Per Master of the Rolls, Heneghan v Manchester Dry Docks and Others [2016] EWCA Civ 86, para 23

INDIVISIBLE OR DIVISIBLE DISEASE?

The next question a practitioner needs to consider is if the disease is divisible or indivisible. Divisible diseases are dose-related, the more exposure the greater the increased risk of harm. Silicosis is a divisible disease.

In disease cases, it is common for there to be many insurance policies covering a period of employment (even where the Claimant was only employed by one Defendant). There will also be cases with multiple Defendants and where there are also non-negligent periods of exposure.

Claims for silicosis will likely be apportioned on a time-exposed basis (as claims for asbestosis are usually determined) and applying a "Holtby discount" for any periods of uninsured exposure or non-negligent exposure. ("Holtby discount" comes from the decision in "Holtby", and in practice means a Claimant accepting they will not recover for periods of exposure where the Defendant is insolvent and there is no policy of insurance).

Questions of exposure will be considered by occupational hygienist/engineering experts, who will often give a variety of scenarios, depending on possible factual outcomes the court may determine. They will often also give an apportionment based on "dose-related exposure.

As seen in the case of Heneghan, lung cancer is an indivisible disease, which exposure to RCS increases the risk of developing. It cannot be apportioned between different causes because medical science is not able to say which exposure caused the cancer. The severity of the disease is not increased by increased exposure; however, the risk of disease does increase in proportion to the amount of RCS inhaled.

In Heneghan, the "double the risk" test was considered more favourably than in Sienkiewicz and it can be foreseen, particularly with developments in medical science, how Defendants (particularly in single exposure cases) may try and argue that their specific period of exposure was so minimal that they should not be held liable (as the Defendants, unsuccessfully did in Sienkiewicz).

It is likely in cases of lung cancer, epidemiological evidence will be utilised to determine the increased risk the exposure to RCS caused. Expert evidence from an occupational hygienist/engineer will be needed to determine the exposure to RCS over an individual's working life and the proportion the Defendants are liable for. Medical evidence will also likely be needed to opine if an inference can be drawn that the level of exposure by an individual Defendant is attributable to RCS exposure.

SOURCES OF EXPOSURE

Finally, a practitioner needs to consider all possible sources of RCS exposure. This includes not only employers/occupiers, but also the client's actions. One can foresee how in certain industries, for example, kitchen fitting, how an individual may have at times been employed and/or worked on large sites where an employer/occupier can be pursued, but they also had periods where they were sole traders/carrying out work on their own home where they were solely responsible for their work (and exposure to RCS) and their conduct will be considered contributory negligent.

Practitioners for Claimants may think that not investigating these issues too much might be better for the client. It might be thought/hoped a Defendant may not argue apportionment. The reality is this is incredibly unlikely and it is far better to establish all sources of RCS exposure (both negligent and non-negligent) so the Claimant can establish their best case. Vague pleadings and witness evidence on these issues, will undoubtedly lead to Part 18 questions by a Defendant rapidly following.

CHAPTER SEVEN

DAMAGES

There are 3 main types of claims for damages for exposure to RCS:

1. Claimant's personal claim for injury, loss and damage (which will be comprised of General Damages – Pain, Suffering and Loss of Amenity and also Special Damages (compensation for past and future financial losses).

2. A claim by the estate of a Deceased Claimant, pursuant to the Law Reform (Miscellaneous Provisions) Act (1934) ("LR(MP)A 1934"), which is for the personal claim the Deceased could have brought in their lifetime.

3. A claim by the dependents of a Deceased Claimant, for loss of dependency, pursuant to the Fatal Accidents Act (1976) ("FAA 1976").

PERSONAL CLAIM BY THE CLAIMANT

GENERAL DAMAGES

A claim for personal injury for exposure to RCS will include, at least a claim for general damages, compensation for the injury suffered. In determining an appropriate award for compensation practitioners and judges will be guided by the Judicial College Guidelines, which at the time of publication were in their 16th Edition.

To prove this head of loss a Claimant will need a report from an appropriate medico-legal expert. In respect to exposure to silicosis, the usual expert to be instructed in respect of medical causation, condition and prognosis will be a respiratory physician, but there also may be a need for other disciplines including psychology/psychiatry.

Claimants are also entitled to interest on general damages (pursuant to s 22 Administration of Justice Act (1969)) from the date of service of the claim form at a rate of 2% until the date of settlement or judgment[48].

SPECIAL DAMAGES

Claimants can also bring claims for special damages, this is compensation for past and future losses. Normal heads of loss include for items such as loss of earnings (if someone has had to retire from work early or reduce hours), care (this can be paid for or gratuitous) and loss of other services (gardening and DIY). A Claimant may need expert evidence (for example from a care expert) to help determine and quantify these heads of loss.

In respect of silicosis and lung cancer a possible area of dispute between parties is claims for future treatment. Medical science is rapidly innovating and developing new treatments for diseases which even 10 years ago were fatal. One particular growth area is immunotherapy, which is a type of treatment which helps activate or suppress the immune system. It is being used in new cancer treatments but is also being trialled in immune diseases such as silicosis.

Pursuant to s 2(4) of the Law Reform (Personal Injuries) Act 1948, a Claimant is entitled to claim for future treatment privately and not make use of NHS availability.

In respect of future treatment, the case of Najib v John Laing Plc [2011] EWHC 1016 QB highlights Claimant's have a relatively low threshold to surmount (particularly in terminal cases) in respect of recoverability. In Najib, a case where the Claimant had mesothelioma, the threshold was

48 Birkett v Hayes [1982] 1 WLR 816

met when the treatment was recommended by a doctor, even though there was no proven benefit.

Immunotherapy is now regularly funded by Defendants in cases of mesothelioma (NICE having approved the use of nivolumab and ipilimumab as first-line treatment for unresectable malignant pleural mesothelioma in 2022). It is yet to be seen if a similar policy will be adopted for lung cancer or silicosis claims arising out of RCS exposure.

PROVISIONAL DAMAGES

In assessing damages the usual approach of the courts is to provide a sum, which is effectively a "once and for all" assessment of future of loss; however, it is ultimately an approximation, and the risk is some Claimants will have a much worse outcome and have been undercompensated, and conversely some Claimants will do much better and be overcompensated.

In respect of many conditions which arise from exposure to RCS such as chronic silicosis, or even COPD, that condition may be of mild-moderate severity and often not fatal; however, both conditions make it more likely for an individual to suffer conditions such as organ failure and tuberculosis which are likely to be much more severe (and therefore with greater special damages, such as care) and possibly fatal. A court faced with a possibility of the development of a serious disease in future (often with the chance of this occurring below 50%) is faced with a difficult position in ensuring a Claimant is fairly compensated.

To overcome this problem s 32A of the Senior Courts Act provides:

> (1) *This section applies to an action for damages for personal injuries in which there is proved or admitted to be a chance that at some definite or indefinite time in the future the injured person will, as a result of the act or omission which gave rise to the cause of*

action, develop some serious disease or suffer some serious deterioration in his physical or mental condition.

(2) Subject to subsection (4) below, as regards any action for damages to which this section applies in which a judgment is given in the High Court, provision may be made by rules of court for enabling the court, in such circumstances as may be prescribed, to award the injured person—

(a) damages assessed on the assumption that the injured person will not develop the disease or suffer the deterioration in his condition; and

(b) further damages at a future date if he develops the disease or suffers the deterioration.

There are also similar provision at s 51 of the County Courts Act 1984. The procedural rules for an order for provisional damages are provided for at CPR 41.2 supported by PD 41 A.

Mrs Justice Hill, in the recent case of Mathieu v Hinds (1) Aviva Plc (2) [2022] EWHC 924 (QB) considered in extensive detail the legal framework in respect of provisional damages:

"The power to award provisional damages was considered by Scott Baker J (as he then was) in Willson v Ministry of Defence [1991] ICR 595. At pp.598H-599A, he identified three questions he had to decide, namely (1) is there a chance of the claimant developing the disease or deterioration in question? (2) is the disease or deterioration serious? and (3) if so, should the court exercise its discretion to make an award of provisional damages? This approach was approved by the Court of Appeal in Curi v Colina , The Times, 14 October 1998: see

> *the judgment of Roch LJ, with whom Ward, and Potter LJ agreed (transcript, p.9)"*[49].

Mrs Justice Hill then went on to consider the questions of chance and seriousness and how in Willson:

> *Scott Baker J considered that the chance must be "measurable rather than fanciful...[h]owever slim" (p.599B-C). The Court of Appeal in Curi held that this was a "sensible and proper approach" and agreed that the chance "must be more than fanciful"*[50].

She then considered how provisional damages can be awarded even when there was a relatively small chance of developing a serious condition (0.1% risk of serious consequences of syringomyelia in the case of Kotula v EDF Energy Networks (EDN) PLC [2011] EWHC 1546 (QB)).

In Mrs Justice Hall's judgment the question of deterioration was fact specific, with the Court of Appeal in Curi v Colina (CA The Times, 14 October 1998):

> *"indicating that a disease or deterioration could be serious because of the effect on the activities, capabilities, life expectancy or financial position of the claimant. Further, the Court held that the disease or deterioration must be "such that an award of damages which included a sum for the 'chance' will be wholly inadequate to compensate the plaintiff for the position in which he would find himself once the chance had materialised"*[51].

[49] [2022] EWHC 924 (QB), 52, para 290

[50] [2022] EWHC 924 (QB), 52, para 291

[51] [2022] EWHC 924 (QB), 52, para 293

In respect of how the court should exercise its discretion in respect of provisional damages, Mrs Justice Hall again cited Scott Baker, J in Willson:

> "*The general rule in English law is that damages are assessed on a once-and-for-all basis. Section 32A of the Supreme Court Act 1981 creates a valuable statutory exception. In my judgment, the section envisages a clear and severable risk rather than a continuing deterioration, as is the typical osteoarthritic picture...many disabilities follow a developing pattern in which the precise results cannot be foreseen. Within a general band this or that may or may not occur. Such are not the cases for provisional damages. The courts have to do their best to make an award in the light of a broad medical prognosis. In my judgment, there should be some clear-cut event which, if it occurs, triggers an entitlement to further compensation*".

He considered that the factors relevant to the exercise of the discretion were:

> "*...first...whether, in respect of any of the three events...there can truly be said to be a clear-cut identifiable threshold...[second] the degree of risk and the consequences of the risk...third...weighing up the possibilities of doing justice by a once-and-for-all assessment against the possibility of doing better justice by reserving the plaintiff's right to return*"[52].

Mrs Justice Hall finally considered the question of causation and cited Slade J who in Chewings v Williams [2010] PIQR Q1 held:

> "*It is for the applicant for a provisional award of damages to establish on a balance of probabilities that there is a chance that at some time in the future he will suffer some serious deterioration in his physical condition. The chance is established by less than a balance of*

[52] [2022] EWHC 924 (QB), 53, para 296

> *probabilities standard. If that standard were satisfied, the event would not be a chance but a certainty not warranting provisional damages but the award of an ascertained sum. There is no warrant for imposing a preliminary hurdle to overcome to a balance of probabilities standard of proof that an event which may lead to deterioration in the applicant's physical condition will occur...the appropriate test to be applied in deciding whether Section 32A is satisfied is whether the claimant has established on a balance of probabilities that as a result of the act or omission which gave rise to the cause of action there is a chance of serious deterioration in his physical condition in the future"*[53].

PD 41, paragraph 2.5, provides that causation of any further damages within the scope of a Provisional Damages order will be determined when any application for further damages is made; however, those drafting Provisional Damage Orders (particularly when a matter has settled) should ensure they take great care to ensure the position in respect of causation is clear in the order. Normally in a Provisional Damages Order there will be a Statement of Facts, which details on what basis the settlement was reached, and in what situation a Claimant can apply for further damages. The need to take great care when drafting these orders was clearly demonstrated in the case of Green v Vickers [2002] EWCA Civ 904, where a claim was settled on a full liability basis, and when the Claimant subsequently died of mesothelioma the Court of Appeal held it was not open for the Defendant to reopen the issue of liability.

A right to apply for Provisional Damages also survives a Claimant's death and passes to the estate[54].

---

53 [2022] EWHC 924 (QB), 55, para 305

54 Power v Bernard Hastie [2002] EWHC 1927

LAW REFORM (MISCELLANEOUS PROVISIONS) ACT 1934 (LR(MP)A 1934)

If a Claimant (or potential Claimant) dies then a claim can be brought, pursuant to LR(MP)A 1934, by the estate for the personal claim that could have been brought in the Deceased's lifetime. Funeral costs can also be claimed where the death was caused by the alleged negligence and the expenses were paid out of the estate. S 4 (2) of the Administration of Justice Act 1982 abolished the survival of a Claimant's estate to bring claims for "lost years".

FATAL ACCIDENT ACT CLAIMS 1976 (FAA 1976)

If a Claimant dies as a result of the Defendant's negligence their dependents can bring a claim under the FAA 1976. 3 types of claims can be brought under FAA 1976:

1. Bereavement

2. Funeral Expenses

3. Claims for loss of income and service dependency

BEREAVEMENT AWARD

At the time of publication, the statutory bereavement award was £15,120. The award is based on the date of death, not the date any claim is made. A limited number of relatives can apply for the bereavement award (spouses, civil partners, parents of a deceased child (but only the Mother if the child is "illegitimate" and minors of a deceased parent if they are unmarried) and only one award can be made.

Given the limited categories, and that only one bereavement award can be made, claims are often made for loss of love and affection as per Regan v Williamson [1976] 1 WLR 205. Such claims when awarded tend to be in the region of a few thousand pounds.

FUNERAL EXPENSES

Pursuant to S 3 (5) FAA 1976 where dependents have incurred funeral expenses, the court may award damages in respect of these cases. The "may" provision has meant in certain cases, particularly where death has been accelerated by a matter of months, the courts refuse to award funeral expenses. Funeral expenses cannot be recovered under the LR(MP)A 1934 and the FAA 1976.

DEPENDENCY CLAIMS FOR LOSS OF INCOME AND SERVICES

Any "dependent" can bring a claim under the FAA 1976 for loss of income and service dependency, there are no statutory restrictions on who can bring a claim. As a general rule of thumb when courts are dealing with loss of income, where there are dependent children in the household the loss will be calculated on the basis of 75% of the Deceased's income. Where there are no dependent children the loss will be calculated on the basis of 66% of the Deceased's income.

CHAPTER EIGHT

LIMITATION

INTRODUCTION

As with many disease claims, in those involving RCS exposure, there is often a latency period between exposure and the development of symptoms (up to 30 years in the case of chronic silicosis). Pursuant to Section 11 (4) of the Limitation Act 1980 (LA 1980) a Claimant has 3 years to bring a claim for personal injury from:

> *(a) the date on which the cause of action accrued; or*
>
> *(b) the date of knowledge (if later) of the person injured.*

If a Claimant dies before the expiration of the period set out in s 11 (4), s 11 (5) provides that by virtue of s 1 of the LR(MP)A 1934 the cause of action, they had for personal injury, survives for three years from:

> *(a) the date of death; or*
>
> *(b) the date of the personal representative's knowledge;*
>
> *whichever is the later.*

Pursuant to the FAA 1976, dependents of a Claimant can also bring a claim for loss of dependency on death. There are special time limits for bringing a claim under this Act as provided by s 12 LA 1980:

> *(1) An action under the Fatal Accidents Act 1976 shall not be brought if the death occurred when the person injured could no longer maintain an action and recover damages in respect of the injury (whether because of a time limit in this Act or in any other Act, or for any other reason).*

Where any such action by the injured person would have been barred by the time limit in section 11 of this Act, no account shall be taken of the possibility of that time limit being overridden under section 33 of this Act.

(2) *None of the time limits given in the preceding provisions of this Act shall apply to an action under the Fatal Accidents Act 1976, but no such action shall be brought after the expiration of three years from*

(a) *the date of death; or*

(b) *the date of knowledge of the person for whose benefit the action is brought;*

whichever is the later.

Very simply if the Deceased had not brought their claim within the 3 years as set out in s 11 LA 1980 (and were still alive and had capacity) at this expiry, then a claim under the FAA cannot be brought, the court does not have the power to disapply the limitation period pursuant to s 33 LA 1980. If the Deceased dies within this 3 year period then dependents have 3 years to bring a claim from the date of death (or if they can prove a later date of knowledge (possibly for example, following a post-mortem)) 3 years from this date. It is very important practitioners are aware of these time limits given that the court's discretion under s 33 LA 1980 does not apply.

DATE OF KNOWLEDGE

As considered earlier in Chapter 6, the ability to bring a claim, where an injury was not discovered until after the standard date of expiration of limitation, was allowed by statute following Cartledge.

In RCS exposure claims, as the cause of action accrues from the time of exposure, but there is often a latency period in respect of symptoms,

Claimant's will often rely on s 11 (4) (b) and aver that their date of knowledge was later.

The recent case of Mr Donald Wilkins v University Hospital North Midlands NHS Trust [2021] EWHC 2164 (QB), helpfully summaries the extensive case law on the date of knowledge in a personal injury claim. Mr Richard Hermer QC sitting as a High Court Judge, referred to the cases of Haward and Other and Fawcetts [2006] 1 WLR 682 and the Supreme Court in AB and Others v Ministry of Defence being the most authoritative source of guidance on this issue and held what was required was:

> *"for a claimant to have the requisite knowledge for the purposes of ss.11 and 14, it is not necessary that they appreciate all the details of the claim that they may later formulate against the Defendant, let alone that there has been an actionable breach of a legal obligation, before time begins to run. Rather, it is sufficient that they understand 'in general terms' the 'essence' of the factual case upon which a later claim might be based. In the context of a clinical negligence claim it is not necessary that the claimant appreciates the precise mechanism by which s/he has sustained an injury but rather it suffices that there is an understanding in broad terms that the medical care may be a possible cause of injury (see the reference to Hendy v Milton Keynes AHA above)[55]".*

In respect of date of knowledge Claimant's medical records will often be a key source of information in particular when the Claimant first reported developing symptoms (which later turned out to be caused by RCS exposure). The test under s 14 (3) LA 1980 is ultimately an objective test and the court can construe a constructive date of knowledge, even where it is accepted, subjectively the Claimant was unaware.

---

[55] [2021] EWHC 2164 (QB), para 51

Where date of knowledge is later then when a date of action accrued this should be pleaded in the Particulars of Claim. Limitation is a defence for a Defendant to raise and in cases where the period is small, a Defendant may choose not to raise the issue.

DISAPPLYING THE PRIMARY LIMITATION PERIOD

Pursuant to s 33 of the Limitation Act 1980, a Claimant can apply to disapply the primary limitation period. The court in exercising its discretion to grant such an application must consider the following factors (as per s 33 (3):

In acting under this section the court shall have regard to all the circumstances of the case and in particular to—

(a) *the length of, and the reasons for, the delay on the part of the plaintiff;*

(b) *the extent to which, having regard to the delay, the evidence adduced or likely to be adduced by the plaintiff or the defendant is or is likely to be less cogent than if the action had been brought within the time allowed by section … or (as the case may be) by section 12;*

(c) *the conduct of the defendant after the cause of action arose, including the extent (if any) to which he responded to requests reasonably made by the plaintiff for information or inspection for the purpose of ascertaining facts which were or might be relevant to the plaintiff's cause of action against the defendant;*

(d) *the duration of any disability of the plaintiff arising after the date of the accrual of the cause of action;*

(e) *the extent to which the plaintiff acted promptly and reasonably once he knew whether or not the act or omission of the defendant, to which the injury was attributable, might be capable at that time of giving rise to an action for damages;*

(f) the steps, if any, taken by the plaintiff to obtain medical, legal or other expert advice and the nature of any such advice he may have received.

Mr Richard Hermer QC (sitting as a High Court Judge) in Wilkins cited the *"authoritative and comprehensive"* guidance of Sir Terence Etherton MR in Carroll v Chief Constable of Manchester [2017] EWCA Civ 1992 in respect of the general principles of how the court should exercise its discretion under section 33 (1)[56]:

"The general principles may be summarised as follows.

1. *Section 33 is not confined to a "residual class of cases". It is unfettered and requires the judge to look at the matter broadly.*

2. *The matters specified in section 33(3) are not intended to place a fetter on the discretion given by section 33(1), as is made plain by the opening words "the court shall have regard to all the circumstances of the case", but to focus the attention of the court on matters which past experience has shown are likely to call for evaluation in the exercise of the discretion and must be taken into a consideration by the judge.*

3. *The essence of the proper exercise of the judicial discretion under section 33 is that the test is a balance of prejudice and the burden is on the claimant to show that his or her prejudice would outweigh that to the defendant. Refusing to exercise the discretion in favour of a claimant who brings the claim outside the primary limitation period will necessarily prejudice the*

[56] Mr Hermer QC removed the case references for clarity to avoid confusion.

claimant, who thereby loses the chance of establishing the claim.

4. *The burden on the claimant under section 33 is not necessarily a heavy one. How heavy or easy it is for the claimant to discharge the burden will depend on the facts of the particular case:*

5. *Furthermore, while the ultimate burden is on a claimant to show that it would be equitable to disapply the statute, the evidential burden of showing that the evidence adduced, or likely to be adduced, by the defendant is, or is likely to be, less cogent because of the delay is on the defendant: If relevant or potentially relevant documentation has been destroyed or lost by the defendant irresponsibly, that is a factor which may weigh against the defendant:*

6. *The prospects of a fair trial are important: The Limitation Acts are designed to protect defendants from the injustice of having to fight stale claims, especially when any witnesses the defendant might have been able to rely on are not available or have no recollection and there are no documents to assist the court in deciding what was done or not done and why: It is, therefore, particularly relevant whether, and to what extent, the defendant's ability to defend the claim has been prejudiced by the lapse of time because of the absence of relevant witnesses and documents.*

7. *Subject to considerations of proportionality (as outlined in para 11 below), the defendant only deserves to have the obligation to pay due damages removed if the passage of time has significantly diminished the opportunity to defend the claim on liability or amount:*

8. *It is the period after the expiry of the limitation period which is referred to in subsubsections 33(3)(a) and (b) and carries particular weight: The court may also, however, have regard to the period of delay from the time at which section 14(2) was satisfied until the claim was first notified: The disappearance of evidence and the loss of cogency of evidence even before the limitation clock starts to tick is also relevant, although to a lesser degree:*

9. *The reason for delay is relevant and may affect the balancing exercise. If it has arisen for an excusable reason, it may be fair and just that the action should proceed despite some unfairness to the defendant due to the delay. If, on the other hand, the reasons for the delay or its length are not good ones, that may tip the balance in the other direction: I consider that the latter may be better expressed by saying that, if there are no good reasons for the delay or its length, there is nothing to qualify or temper the prejudice which has been caused to the defendant by the effect of the delay on the defendant's ability to defend the claim.*

10. *Delay caused by the conduct of the claimant's advisers rather than by the claimant may be excusable in this context:*

11. *In the context of reasons for delay, it is relevant to consider under subsection 33(3)(a) whether knowledge or information was reasonably suppressed by the claimant which, if not suppressed, would have led to the proceedings being issued earlier, even though the explanation is irrelevant for meeting the objective standard or test in section 14(2) and (3) and so insufficient to prevent the commencement of the limitation period:*

12. *Proportionality is material to the exercise of the discretion: In that context, it may be relevant that the claim has only a thin*

> *prospect of success, that the claim is modest in financial terms so as to give rise to disproportionate legal costs, that the claimant would have a clear case against his or her solicitors and, in a personal injury case, the extent and degree of damage to the claimant's health, enjoyment of life and employability"*[57].

As per the above guidance, the proper exercise of the judicial discretion in such an application is a balancing exercise in respect of prejudice to the parties. Each case will be fact specific. Cases in which the delay has been short and there appears to be little impact on cogency are far more likely to succeed then in cases where the passage of time has meant there are little records for the time and/or witnesses and places the Defendant at a severe disadvantage in defending the claim.

PRELIMINARY ISSUE

Where limitation is raised as a defence, different courts take different views on if the matter should be dealt with as a preliminary issue. Some courts routinely list for a preliminary hearing all disease cases where limitation is raised, and other courts consider if such a hearing is needed on a case-by-case basis, including the views of the parties expressed in their Direction Questionnaires.

[57] [2021] EHC 2164 (QB), para 59

CHAPTER NINE

PRE-LITIGATION

IDENTIFYING THE CORRECT DEFENDANT

Companies, while from the perspective of the Claimant remain the same organisation, will often have had various changes in the name of their legal entity during a Claimant's employment. The correct identity of a Claimant's employer (and any changes in legal entity during this period) can easily be established by obtaining a Claimant's employment records from HMRC.

Since 1969 it has been compulsory for employers in Great Britain to insure and maintain insurance against liability for bodily injuries or disease sustained by employees in the course of their employment[58]. Whilst a Claimant brings a claim against their former employer it will usually be the Insurer who will be liable to ultimately compensate, in the event of the Claimant obtaining a settlement/judgment (subject to the size of any excess held by the insured on a policy of insurance). There may be several different policies of insurance (and Insurers) covering a Claimant's period of employment.

Given the long latency period for chronic silicosis (10 – 30 years), it will not be uncommon (as with many other disease claims) for former employers to have been dissolved, and it will be the Insurer(s) who will in fact be defending the claim. In 2011 the Employers' Liability Tracing Office was launched to give Claimants easy access to their employer's

[58] Employers' Liability (Compulsory Insurance) Act 1969

liability insurance data. Despite this Office, it is not unusual for there to be periods of employment (especially in dissolved companies) where an Insurer and a relevant policy of insurance cannot be identified.

As will be detailed in the next chapter, where a Defendant employer is in fact a dissolved company certain steps must be taken to ensure the claim is brought against a legal entity.

PRE-ACTION PROTOCOL FOR DISEASE AND ILLNESS CLAIMS

Pre-action conduct should follow the Pre-Action Protocol for Disease and Illness Claims (save for claims under £25,000 with only one Defendant). Failure to comply with the Protocol can be taken into account in any subsequent court proceedings and lead to costs consequences for the defaulting party.

Pre-Action protocols arose as part of the Lord Woolf Reforms. The aim of the protocols is to encourage early contact between parties, early exchange of information, a much more "cards on the table" approach to litigation, to enable early and fair settlement if that is appropriate, and in cases which proceed to litigation ensure this runs efficiently.

The Protocol encourages early disclosure of documentation held by both parties (including medical records) and for the Claimant to put forward their allegations early in a Letter of Claim (Paragraph 6) and for the Defendant to provide their position by way of a Letter of Reponses (Paragraph 7).

The Protocol recognises in disease claims, expert evidence may be needed on various issues including: knowledge, fault, causation, apportionment, condition and prognosis and valuing the claim (Paragraph 9.1). The Protocol, while reminding the parties that the CPR encourages economy in the use of experts, recognises that in disease claims there will need to be flexibility in respect of the approach to expert evidence (Paragraph 9.2).

Despite the apparent flexibility of the Protocol, practitioners should be aware of the courts duty under CPR 35.1 to restrict expert evidence to that which is reasonably required to resolve the proceedings. Just because a party obtains expert evidence does not mean if the matter litigates the court will give permission for this to be relied on. When parties both have experts in the same discipline this increases costs (not only from the reports, but the need for joint statements and also the length of trial). Particularly in low value cases, the court's starting point in respect of occupational hygiene evidence is likely to be joint instruction by the parties.

Chapters 5 and 7 have considered expert evidence in more detail. The Protocol gives detailed guidance on obtaining such evidence, including trying to agree single experts. The first expert evidence the Claimant will likely obtain is in respect of medical causation, condition and prognosis. The Claimant will require this evidence to confirm they have suffered an injury caused by RCS exposure. Covid-19 has caused huge delays in obtaining expert reports, with many experts not taking new instructions in order to deal with claims they had already accepted prior to the pandemic. This is a particular problem in respect of experts in respiratory health who were in extreme demand during the pandemic. Parties need to be aware of these delays in respect of obtaining evidence and also in respect of realistic directions for the trial timetable.

Where a Defendant admits liability in whole, or in part, before proceedings are issued, Part 9.11 of the Protocol states any medical report obtained by the Claimant should be disclosed to the other party.

Witness evidence has been considered in detail in Chapters 5 in and 7, but it is good practice for practitioners (both Claimants and Defendants) to look at obtaining witness evidence as soon as possible. Memories have a tendency to fade as time passes and so the closer evidence can be written down to the event the better. In respect of Claimants, practitioners might be dealing with individuals who are terminally ill, in which case there will be an urgent need to obtain a signed CPR 32 compliant witness statement as soon as possible. While courts will have great sympathy for families bringing claims on behalf of a Deceased Claimant, it is still for the Claimant to prove their case, and in the absence of witness evidence from the Claimant this can be incredibly difficult. (Even where such statements are obtained, there will be arguments about what weight that can be attached to such statements because of the inability to cross-examine).

Part 10 of the Protocol reminds parties that Part 36 offers can be made pre-action, and they are encouraged to consider making such offers. With the changes to QOCS from 1 April 2023, there is a greater incentive on Defendant's to make early Part 36 offers (as they will be able to enforce their costs if the Claimant accepts the offer late, or they beat the offer at trial, not only against the Claimant's damages, but also their costs).

LOW VALUE DISEASE CLAIMS

Where a claim for RCS exposure is valued under £25,000, and there is one Defendant, it should be started in the Pre-Action Protocol for Low-Value Personal Injury (Employers' Liability and Public Liability) Claims. Colloquially known as "the Portal", the aim of the Protocol is to ensure Defendants pay damages and cost set out in the Protocol without Claimant's needing to start proceedings (Part 3.1 (1)). The Protocol allows only fixed costs. The Portal is all online and requires Defendants to quickly confirm if they intend to dispute liability. There are specific time frames for actions to be performed and if they are not, or a Defendant denies liability, the matter "falls" out of the Portal. Unlike other EL/PL claims, after dropping out of the Portal, disease claims are no longer governed by the fixed cost provisions under CPR 45.

CHAPTER TEN

LITIGATION PROCEDURE

ISSUING THE CLAIM – CORRECT DEFENDANT

While a Claimant may have worked for only one employer, there in fact may be several policies of insurance and Insurers covering this period of employment. In respect of disease claims, many Insurers have Memorandums of Understanding or Agreements where they act as one entity for defending the claim, and if a settlement is agreed upon, or judgment awarded, the respective contributions are decided between the Insurers.

As detailed in the last chapter, often in disease claims, the former employer will be dissolved and is no longer on the Register at Companies House. Even when there is an Insurer who has accepted that they issued a policy of insurance for the relevant period (or part of it) and effectively has stepped into the shoes of the employer to defend the action, it must be remembered the claim must be brought against a valid legal entity.

Where a Defendant is no longer on the Register at Companies House a Claimant can either:

- apply to restore a company to the Register; or

- bring an action directly against an insurer of insolvent persons, pursuant to Third Parties (Rights against Insurers) Act 2010. The Act allows a third party to bring a direct action against an insurer, where they reasonably believe: (i) the insured has incurred a liability to them and (ii) the insurer holds a policy of insurance for that liability.

Often where there are multiple material insurance policies, but the insurers have agreed to co-operate for the purposes of defending the claim, an application to restore the insolvent company to the Register is the best course of action, rather than the Claimant bringing the claim against multiple insurers.

If a Claimant fails to restore a company to the Register before issuing proceedings, then often parties will agree the matter shall be stayed for an application to restore to be made. Where such an application is made, and a company is restored to the Register, pursuant to Peakstone Ltd v Joddrell [2013] 1 WLR 784 service of the claim can be retrospectively validated.

While service can be retrospectively validated, the case of Cowley v LW Carlisle and Company Ltd [2020] EWCA Civ 227 should act as a cautionary tale. The Claimant brought a claim for Noise Induce Hearing Loss, but had failed to restore to the company to the Register. The Defendant applied for the claim to be struck out. At the application hearing, the Claimant submitted that the company would be imminently restored to the Register; however, no evidence had been submitted to this effect at the time of the application. The claim was struck out by the District Judge and the decision was upheld on appeal.

PART 18 QUESTIONS

It is not unusual in disease claims for Part 18 questions to be placed to a Claimant following service of the Particulars of Claim (however, CPR 18 allows the court to order them at any time against any party). When posed to Claimants in disease claims, questions will often focus on providing further details of where and how the Claimant worked and also the development of symptoms. CPR 18.1 provides that the questions should:

> *(a) clarify any matter which is in dispute in the proceedings; or*

> *(b) give additional information in relation to any such matter,*
>
> *whether or not the matter is contained or referred to in a statement of case.*

Claimants will often oppose such applications, arguing that the questions will be answered by way of disclosure of medical records or within a witness statement; however, while courts will not allow Part 18s to be used as cross-examination, they are generally keen for matters to be clarified in order for both parties to understand the other sides' claim.

DIRECTION QUESTIONNAIRES

Once both parties have filed and served their pleadings, the court will require them to complete Directions Questionnaires ("DQs"). These DQs will be then be reviewed by normally the District Judge bench in county court cases and High Court District Registries, and by the Masters in the High Court in London. The matters may be listed for allocation and directions hearings, or in lower value claims, the court may just make a directions order. Where matters are, or are likely to, be allocated to the Multi-Track the court will list the matter for a Cost and Case Management Hearing.

It is therefore important parties carefully complete the DQ indicating the track they believe is appropriate, the need for expert evidence, number of witnesses and also trial length. Where a direction is sought which is outside "standard directions", for example several experts on a Fast Track Trial, the parties should provide adequate information of why this is needed.

Matters allocated to the Fast Track will often be given "standard directions" by the court. Parties should be careful to check the directions. They have 7 days after the order was served on them to make an application to vary any order (CPR 3 (5)).

DISCLOSURE

If the parties have complied with the Pre-Action Protocol for Disease and Illness Claims the majority of disclosure should have occurred before the claim is litigated. The court will still likely order disclosure by list, but any further disclosure, at this stage, will predominantly be updating records.

WITNESS EVIDENCE

In Chapters 5, 7 and 9 the requirements for witness evidence were considered in detail. If all matters are being dealt with in a final hearing (limitation, negligence and quantum) witness evidence will need to deal with all these issues. Heads of loss like gratuitous care (which is held on Trust for the person who provides the actual care) should be evidenced, as far as possible, by a supporting statement from the person who actually provided the care[59].

EXPERT EVIDENCE

The need for expert evidence was considered in Chapters 5, 7 and 9. In RCS exposure cases it is likely that parties will both be allowed their own medical evidence (save for possibly in very low value cases) and engineering evidence will be required. If both parties will be given permission for this discipline, or if the court will order joint instruction, will depend on the complexity of the issues in the case and value.

The Civil Justice Council has provided detailed guidance entitled: Guidance for the instruction of experts in civil claims[60], which covers

---

59 Hunt v Severs [1994] 2 AC 350 HL

https://www.judiciary.uk/wp-content/uploads/2014/08/experts-guidance-cjc-aug-2014-amended-dec-8.pdf everything from the need for experts, attendance of experts at court and payment.

Often if the court only allows one party (usually the Claimant) to rely on an expert in a certain discipline the other party will be given provision to ask questions of that expert. CPR 35.6 deals with questions to an expert and provides they should only be asked once (CPR 35.6 (2) (a) and within 28 days of service of an expert's report (CPR 35.6 (2) (b)), unless the court gives permission or the other side agrees (CPR 35.6 (c) (i) and (ii)). It is normal for the court to give a party permission to ask questions of an expert once disclosure and witness evidence has been completed (particularly in respect of medical evidence).

CPR 35.6 requires any questions to be asked to be proportionate, in particular they should not be a cross-examination of the expert, but a way of exploring and clarifying their opinion. Where questions are excessive and disproportionate a party can apply for them to be disallowed. In Mustard v Flower and Ors [2019] EWHC 2623 (QB), Master Davison disallowed lengthy and complex questions posed by the Claimant to the Defendant's experts. As an example, in respect of the neuropsychology evidence, there were 47 discrete questions asked, which contained various sub-parts. Master Davison commented:

> *"I have never encountered a set of questions to experts even remotely approaching the scale and complexity of these"*[61].

Where the Court gives permission of both parties to rely on their own expert, the experts in the same discipline will need to meet to produce a joint statement. A continuing problem is agreeing Agendas, with may parties using them as a cross-examination, rather than an aid for the experts to identify and discuss the issues, where possible reach an agreed opinion and where they disagree the reasons for disagreement (CPR 35.12 (1)(a), (b) and (3)(b)).

[61] [2019] EWHC 2623 (QB)

The consequence is often a lack of agreement between the parties on agendas and 2 being produced and sent to experts. Mrs Justice Yip, in both the case of Saunders v Central Manchester University Hospital NHS Foundation Trust [2018] EWHC 343 (QB) and Welsh v Wallsall Healthcare NHS Trust [2018] EWHC 1917 (QB), has warned parties the court may impose cost consequences if the trend for 2 agendas continues. She reminded parties:

> *"Parties should adopt a common sense and collaborative approach rather than allowing this stage of the litigation to become a battleground"*[62].

CPR 35.12, and the supporting PD at paragraph 9, set out the rules for joint discussions. Importantly, the actual discussion cannot be referred to at trial (CPR 35.12.(4)). Experts are reminded they must give their own opinion and do not need the authority of the party that instructed them to sign a joint statement (PD paragraph 9.7). If an expert significantly alters their view in the joint statement they should record the reason for doing so in a note or addendum (PD paragraph 9.8).

CONFERENCE WITH WITNESS AND EXPERTS

Conferences with witnesses and experts can be vital in respect of case preparation and help the parties see the relative strengthens and weakness in their case – they are not for legal representatives to coach either lay or expert witnesses on what to say.

There are strict rules for both solicitors and barristers in respect of witness preparation. The Bar Standards Board Handbook, Rule C9.4, has a fundamental prohibition on rehearsing, practising or coaching a witness.

[62] Saunders v Central Manchester University Hospital NHS Foundation Trust [2018] EWHC 343 (QB), para 35.

The timing of conferences is important. Courts will not allow endless conferences, they may, depending on the size of case only budget for one. Practitioners will therefore have to consider when to use this budget most effectively, which will undoubtedly depend on each case.

TRIAL

Only around 5% of Personal Injuries cases go to trial and many are on limited issues (for example limitation); however, even with those statistics it is important to ensure witnesses (both lay and expert) are available to attend trial. In cases in the County Court, the need for oral expert evidence, will normally not be given automatically and need to be applied for at the Pre-Trial Checklist stage or before. In the High Court, it is normally given, but parties may still agree certain disciplines (or even all experts) do not need to attend.

Preparation for, and attendance at trial, can be stressful for both witnesses and practitioners (expert witnesses can usually count on their hands the times they have actually had to attend trial to give expert evidence and for many lay witnesses it can be their first-time attending court). Attention to small details (ensuring everyone has contact numbers if something goes wrong on the day, making sure you know where you are going to park if you are driving to court, arriving early so you can have a pre-trial conference) can help reduce the stress.

While there was a move to remote hearings during the pandemic, more and more courts are dealing with trials in person; however, if a trial is heard remotely, practitioners must ensure all witnesses have a clean copy of the bundle and also appropriate facilities to attend the hearing. Where you have concerns about a witnesses' technology, it may be sensible for them to attend remotely from instructing Solicitor's Office or Counsel's Chambers.

CONCLUSION

This guide has been intended to be a very high-level overview in prosecuting and defending RCS exposure claims. As mentioned right at the start of this book, this is an area where there are predictions of increased litigation. While historically cases have been brought for RCS exposure (and are authoritative guidance in respect of causation in disease cases), less claims have been brought recently. As more claims for RCS exposure are litigated, more modern case law will become available, and practitioners are encouraged to keep abreast of new developments in this area of law.

MORE BOOKS BY LAW BRIEF PUBLISHING

A selection of our other titles available now:-

'A Practical Guide to Parental Alienation in Private and Public Law Children Cases' by Sam King QC & Frankie Shama
'Contested Heritage – Removing Art from Land and Historic Buildings' by Richard Harwood QC, Catherine Dobson, David Sawtell
'The Limits of Separate Legal Personality: When Those Running a Company Can Be Held Personally Liable for Losses Caused to Third Parties Outside of the Company' by Dr Mike Wilkinson
'A Practical Guide to Transgender Law' by Robin Moira White & Nicola Newbegin
'Artificial Intelligence – The Practical Legal Issues (2nd Edition)' by John Buyers
'A Practical Guide to Residential Freehold Conveyancing' by Lorraine Richardson
'A Practical Guide to Pensions on Divorce for Lawyers' by Bryan Scant
'A Practical Guide to Challenging Sham Marriage Allegations in Immigration Law' by Priya Solanki
'A Practical Guide to Legal Rights in Scotland' by Sarah-Jane Macdonald
'A Practical Guide to New Build Conveyancing' by Paul Sams & Rebecca East
'A Practical Guide to Defending Barristers in Disciplinary Cases' by Marc Beaumont
'A Practical Guide to Inherited Wealth on Divorce' by Hayley Trim
'A Practical Guide to Practice Direction 12J and Domestic Abuse in Private Law Children Proceedings' by Rebecca Cross & Malvika Jaganmohan
'A Practical Guide to Confiscation and Restraint' by Narita Bahra QC, John Carl Townsend, David Winch
'A Practical Guide to the Law of Forests in Scotland' by Philip Buchan
'A Practical Guide to Health and Medical Cases in Immigration Law' by Rebecca Chapman & Miranda Butler
'A Practical Guide to Bad Character Evidence for Criminal Practitioners by Aparna Rao
'A Practical Guide to Extradition Law post-Brexit' by Myles Grandison et al

'A Practical Guide to Hoarding and Mental Health for Housing Lawyers' by Rachel Coyle
'A Practical Guide to Psychiatric Claims in Personal Injury – 2nd Edition' by Liam Ryan
'Stephens on Contractual Indemnities' by Richard Stephens
'A Practical Guide to the EU Succession Regulation' by Richard Frimston
'A Practical Guide to Solicitor and Client Costs – 2nd Edition' by Robin Dunne
'Constructive Dismissal – Practice Pointers and Principles' by Benjimin Burgher
'A Practical Guide to Religion and Belief Discrimination Claims in the Workplace' by Kashif Ali
'A Practical Guide to the Law of Medical Treatment Decisions' by Ben Troke
'Fundamental Dishonesty and QOCS in Personal Injury Proceedings: Law and Practice' by Jake Rowley
'A Practical Guide to the Law in Relation to School Exclusions' by Charlotte Hadfield & Alice de Coverley
'A Practical Guide to Divorce for the Silver Separators' by Karin Walker
'The Right to be Forgotten – The Law and Practical Issues' by Melissa Stock
'A Practical Guide to Planning Law and Rights of Way in National Parks, the Broads and AONBs' by James Maurici QC, James Neill et al
'A Practical Guide to Election Law' by Tom Tabori
'A Practical Guide to the Law in Relation to Surrogacy' by Andrew Powell
'A Practical Guide to Claims Arising from Fatal Accidents – 2nd Edition' by James Patience
'A Practical Guide to the Ownership of Employee Inventions – From Entitlement to Compensation' by James Tumbridge & Ashley Roughton
'A Practical Guide to Asbestos Claims' by Jonathan Owen & Gareth McAloon
'A Practical Guide to Stamp Duty Land Tax in England and Northern Ireland' by Suzanne O'Hara
'A Practical Guide to the Law of Farming Partnerships' by Philip Whitcomb
'Covid-19, Homeworking and the Law – The Essential Guide to Employment and GDPR Issues' by Forbes Solicitors
'Covid-19 and Criminal Law – The Essential Guide' by Ramya Nagesh
'Covid-19 and Family Law in England and Wales – The Essential Guide' by Safda Mahmood

'A Practical Guide to the Law of Unlawful Eviction and Harassment – 2nd Edition' by Stephanie Lovegrove
'Covid-19, Brexit and the Law of Commercial Leases – The Essential Guide' by Mark Shelton
'A Practical Guide to Costs in Personal Injury Claims – 2nd Edition' by Matthew Hoe
'A Practical Guide to the General Data Protection Regulation (GDPR) – 2nd Edition' by Keith Markham
'Ellis on Credit Hire – Sixth Edition' by Aidan Ellis & Tim Kevan
'A Practical Guide to Working with Litigants in Person and McKenzie Friends in Family Cases' by Stuart Barlow
'Protecting Unregistered Brands: A Practical Guide to the Law of Passing Off' by Lorna Brazell
'A Practical Guide to Secondary Liability and Joint Enterprise Post-Jogee' by Joanne Cecil & James Mehigan
'A Practical Guide to the Pre-Action RTA Claims Protocol for Personal Injury Lawyers' by Antonia Ford
'A Practical Guide to Neighbour Disputes and the Law' by Alexander Walsh
'A Practical Guide to Forfeiture of Leases' by Mark Shelton
'A Practical Guide to Coercive Control for Legal Practitioners and Victims' by Rachel Horman
'A Practical Guide to Rights Over Airspace and Subsoil' by Daniel Gatty
'Tackling Disclosure in the Criminal Courts – A Practitioner's Guide' by Narita Bahra QC & Don Ramble
'A Practical Guide to the Law of Driverless Cars – Second Edition' by Alex Glassbrook, Emma Northey & Scarlett Milligan
'A Practical Guide to TOLATA Claims' by Greg Williams
'A Practical Guide to Elderly Law – 2nd Edition' by Justin Patten
'A Practical Guide to Responding to Housing Disrepair and Unfitness Claims' by Iain Wightwick
'A Practical Guide to the Construction and Rectification of Wills and Trust Instruments' by Edward Hewitt
'A Practical Guide to the Law of Bullying and Harassment in the Workplace' by Philip Hyland
'How to Be a Freelance Solicitor: A Practical Guide to the SRA-Regulated Freelance Solicitor Model' by Paul Bennett

'A Practical Guide to Prison Injury Claims' by Malcolm Johnson
'A Practical Guide to the Small Claims Track - 2nd Edition' by Dominic Bright
'A Practical Guide to Advising Clients at the Police Station' by Colin Stephen McKeown-Beaumont
'A Practical Guide to Antisocial Behaviour Injunctions' by Iain Wightwick
'Practical Mediation: A Guide for Mediators, Advocates, Advisers, Lawyers, and Students in Civil, Commercial, Business, Property, Workplace, and Employment Cases' by Jonathan Dingle with John Sephton
'The Mini-Pupillage Workbook' by David Boyle
'A Practical Guide to Crofting Law' by Brian Inkster
'A Practical Guide to Spousal Maintenance' by Liz Cowell
'A Practical Guide to the Law of Domain Names and Cybersquatting' by Andrew Clemson
'A Practical Guide to the Law of Gender Pay Gap Reporting' by Harini Iyengar
'A Practical Guide to the Rights of Grandparents in Children Proceedings' by Stuart Barlow
'NHS Whistleblowing and the Law' by Joseph England
'Employment Law and the Gig Economy' by Nigel Mackay & Annie Powell
'A Practical Guide to Noise Induced Hearing Loss (NIHL) Claims' by Andrew Mckie, Ian Skeate, Gareth McAloon
'An Introduction to Beauty Negligence Claims – A Practical Guide for the Personal Injury Practitioner' by Greg Almond
'Intercompany Agreements for Transfer Pricing Compliance' by Paul Sutton
'Zen and the Art of Mediation' by Martin Plowman
'A Practical Guide to the SRA Principles, Individual and Law Firm Codes of Conduct 2019 – What Every Law Firm Needs to Know' by Paul Bennett
'A Practical Guide to Adoption for Family Lawyers' by Graham Pegg
'A Practical Guide to Industrial Disease Claims' by Andrew Mckie & Ian Skeate
'A Practical Guide to Redundancy' by Philip Hyland
'A Practical Guide to Vicarious Liability' by Mariel Irvine
'A Practical Guide to Applications for Landlord's Consent and Variation of Leases' by Mark Shelton
'A Practical Guide to Relief from Sanctions Post-Mitchell and Denton' by Peter Causton

'A Practical Guide to Equity Release for Advisors' by Paul Sams
'A Practical Guide to Financial Services Claims' by Chris Hegarty
'The Law of Houses in Multiple Occupation: A Practical Guide to HMO Proceedings' by Julian Hunt
'Occupiers, Highways and Defective Premises Claims: A Practical Guide Post-Jackson – 2nd Edition' by Andrew Mckie
'A Practical Guide to Financial Ombudsman Service Claims' by Adam Temple & Robert Scrivenor
'A Practical Guide to Advising Schools on Employment Law' by Jonathan Holden
'A Practical Guide to Running Housing Disrepair and Cavity Wall Claims: 2nd Edition' by Andrew Mckie & Ian Skeate
'A Practical Guide to Holiday Sickness Claims – 2nd Edition' by Andrew Mckie & Ian Skeate
'Arguments and Tactics for Personal Injury and Clinical Negligence Claims' by Dorian Williams
'A Practical Guide to Drone Law' by Rufus Ballaster, Andrew Firman, Eleanor Clot
'A Practical Guide to Compliance for Personal Injury Firms Working With Claims Management Companies' by Paul Bennett
'RTA Allegations of Fraud in a Post-Jackson Era: The Handbook – 2nd Edition' by Andrew Mckie
'RTA Personal Injury Claims: A Practical Guide Post-Jackson' by Andrew Mckie
'On Experts: CPR35 for Lawyers and Experts' by David Boyle
'An Introduction to Personal Injury Law' by David Boyle

These books and more are available to order online direct from the publisher at www.lawbriefpublishing.com, where you can also read free sample chapters. For any queries, contact us on 0844 587 2383 or mail@lawbriefpublishing.com.

Our books are also usually in stock at www.amazon.co.uk with free next day delivery for Prime members, and at good legal bookshops such as Wildy & Sons.

We are regularly launching new books in our series of practical day-to-day practitioners' guides. Visit our website and join our free newsletter to be kept informed and to receive special offers, free chapters, etc.

You can also follow us on Twitter at www.twitter.com/lawbriefpub.

www.ingramcontent.com/pod-product-compliance
Ingram Content Group UK Ltd.
Pitfield, Milton Keynes, MK11 3LW, UK
UKHW020150290926
15471UKWH00004B/784

9 781914 608728